RAVING REFERRALS

THE PROVEN STEP-BY-STEP SYSTEM

TO

ATTRACT PROFITABLE PROSPECTS

BRANDON BARNUM

CEO OF HOA.COM

Goodyear, AZ

Raving Referral – The Proven Step-by-Step System to Attract Profitable Prospects

Paperback ISBN: 978-1-953806-59-8
Hardcover ISBN: 978-1-953806-60-4
eBook ISBN: 978-1-953806-61-1

Library of Congress Control Number: 2021916463

Publisher: The Champion Institute
Assisting Publisher: Spotlight Publishing™ https://spotlightpublishing.pro
Main Editor: Becky Norwood
Interior Design: Amit Dey

Connect with Brandon Barnum
Email: brandon@ravingreferrals.com
Web: www.RavingReferrals.com
LinkedIn: www.linkedin.com/in/brandonbarnum/

Raving Referrals Endorsements

"If you want more income, influence, and impact, Brandon Barnum's new Raving Referrals book teaches what you need to succeed."

—Mark Victor Hansen

– World's #1 best-selling non-fiction author
– Chicken Soup For The Soul

"Raving Referrals by Brandon Barnum provides the best strategies and tactics for learning how to ASK for and GET those referrals. Understanding your referral score, adopting the 7 laws of raving referrals and measuring referral lifetime client value are a few of the key concepts you'll learn in this idea-packed book. There is nothing more valuable to your career, business and team survival than getting great referrals. Start reading Raving Referrals today and be sure to purchase enough copies for your entire team!"

—Dave Savage – CEO of Mortgage Coach

"Buy this book now. You'll attract more referrals, win more business, and take it to the BANK!"

—Cheri Tree – CEO of Codebreaker Technologies

"Shows business owners and sales professionals how to create consistent clients with predictable profitability."

—Gail Watson
– CEO of Women Speakers Association

"This book gives you a practical and proven process to attract an endless stream of profitable prospects."

—Emmeline Saavedra
– President of The Champions Institute

"Brandon Barnum's book 'Raving Referrals' has been one of the most impactful books I have ever read. I operate my business exclusively from word-of-mouth referrals. I have always been skilled at naturally building and maintaining solid relationships that focus on win-win partnerships. What I didn't have was the systems and processes that would allow me to scale those abilities to an infinite level. Brandon's book is the perfect guide if you are looking to build an endless referral business. I was completely blown away by each chapter and how detailed it was in regard to building the perfect referral systems. This is a book that I will reread at least twice a year."

—Kyle Fuller
– CEO of Factum Financial

"WOW. I've known Brandon for over 20 years, but the guy continues to amaze me with his creativity and ability to connect good people (like us!!!) for the greater good. Raving Referrals is a treasure trove of people and resources to help each of us up our game."

—Tom Crawford
- Founder of Telehealth Partners

"Brandon Barnum's new book Raving Referrals is powerful, precise, and practical. Highly recommend it. You're going to love it."

—Craig Shelley
– COO of IMPACT Realty Tampa Bay

"This book provides a virtual roadmap of how to build a referral system for your business."

—David Baer
– Marketing Strategist of The Prepared Group

"When you incorporate the valuable information in this book, you'll find that you'll win more sales, do it in less time, and build a strong base of lifetime customers who will act as sources of raving referrals."

—Dr. Tony Alessandra - Author of *The Platinum Rule for Sales Mastery* & *Room Full of Referrals*

"Raving Referrals holds the secrets and strategies to gain your most ideal prospects from existing clients and business partners. Jump to the front of the line with referrals that easily convert with the know, like and trust factor!"

—Debbie Allen
- Bestselling Author of *The Highly Paid Expert*

"If you want an endless stream of referrals to your business a proven system is mandatory. This book gives you the best possible framework available to increase both your revenue and your profits."

—Michael Harris – Business Coach

“I’ve built my business on referrals, so I thought I had a good referral game going on. However, as I dived deeper in Raving Referrals, I realized that my Referral Score was pretty low! This book is packed full of advice and actionable concepts, but my favorite is chapter 1, "What's your Referral Score?" What an awesome concept! Numbers are telling and separate fact from fiction, (aka, what we think we're doing, vs. what we're actually doing). Bottom line, there's so much more I can do to up my referral game. Thanks, Brandon, for sharing this wisdom with the world.”

—Beejel Parmar
– Founder of BeeEPIC Outsourcing

“Thank you so much for writing your book “Raving Referrals”. This is going to help so many people master the art of getting referrals for their business with your simple strategies and principles.”

—Tisha Pelletier
– Personal Branding Expert

“Raving Referrals provides the exact marketing and sales blueprint every business owner needs for growing a successful and sustainable business, while creating massive impact. Proven, practical and actionable - this book should be in every business owner’s toolkit!”

—Michela Quilici
– Business Growth Strategist

Congratulations and thank you for getting this Raving Referrals book. Scan the QR code below to view a special video welcome message:

Dedication

I dedicate my life to glorifying God every day in every way. We are all blessed to live in a world with unlimited possibilities, and God, our creator, wants to co-create with you. I invite you to turn to Him and ASK for everything you want in life. Spend time in gratitude and prayer ASKing God to guide your life journey. As you invite God in and shine His light through your life, you will experience miracles and magic that lead to a life well-lived.

While my life is dedicated to God, this book is dedicated to my wife, Marlo, without whom none of my success would be possible. Marlo, you have stood by my side, supporting my dreams and aspirations for 28 years. I have watched you grow, mature, and evolve into an incredible person I am proud to call my wife for life.

Acknowledgments

While there are so many people to thank for bringing this book to be, the most significant acknowledgment goes out to my friend and mentor, Mark Victor Hansen. Since meeting Mark on May 18, 2004, he has constantly elevated and expanded my thinking of what's possible. Over the past 17 years, Mark has taught me that anything I desire and ask for can be achieved.

While he's only halfway to his goal of selling a billion books, the impact Mark has made on the world through Chicken Soup for the Soul, The One Minute Millionaire, and his other best-selling books, and he is well on his way to "make the world work for 100 percent of humanity."

In my life, family always comes first. I've been blessed to not only have an amazing wife to share the last 28 years with, but also three amazing kids that has given my life meaning and fulfillment. Sebastian, you are a brilliant man who has taught me so much and helped dramatically expand my view of the world. Thanks for teaching me what it takes to be a dad and accepting me for living in Wonkaland. Jackson, you are a natural leader and I look forward to seeing where your journey takes you.

Regardless of the destination, I know you and everyone around you will enjoy the ride. Ella, you are so intelligent, talented, driven, and creative. You've grown so much these past few years and the best is yet to come. Your mom and I will be cheering you all on as you explore this adventure called life.

Of course, family would not be complete without the wise ones who taught us what we know. Mom, thanks for your unconditional love, endless optimism, and for holding your vision for the future you want for the world. I so admire your relentless belief in the best for all humanity and look forward to celebrating the great transition with you in the near future. Gayle and Don, you are amazing parents who have given so much love and support to your girls. You exemplify love in action, and I hope you know that the ripple effect of your caring and support is beyond measure.

Contributors

This book came to be thanks to the passionate support of Emmie & Wil Saavedra whom I am beyond grateful to have as both business partners as well as friends. We have so much impact and empowerment to create, and I am thrilled we are doing it together. A special thanks to Audra Boyd, Christian Lumapay, and John Villanueva with The Champions Institute for helping refine and improve this Raving Referrals book, curriculum, and course. I'm also grateful for the support and partnership of Thomas Evans, Justin Banks and Spencer Hesseltine from HOA.com who are always in the lab with me testing and perfecting the referral partner process and co-marketing campaigns. Lastly, I'm so grateful to have been referred to Becky Norwood with Spotlight Publishing whose support and coaching has been extremely empowering. Thanks for making this book and dream, a reality.

I am also grateful to the following experts and influencers who said YES to sharing their brilliance with the Raving Referrals community. Your participation, partnership and friendship are appreciated more than you know.

Aaron Young	Chairman of Laughlin Associates
Adrien Chenault	CEO of Contact Mapping
Allison H. Larsen	Founder of The Speakers Coalition
Ann DeVere	Producer of Access to Expert TV

Barbara Wainright	CEO of Wainwright Global
Becky Norwood	CEO of Spotlight Publishing
Beejel Parmar	Co-Founder of The Process Hive
Burke Franklin	CEO & Founder BusinessPowerTools.com
Carol Dysart	Founder of People Smart Enterprises
Casey Eberhart	CEO of The Ideal Networker
Cheri Tree	CEO of Codebreaker Technologies
Cori Michael-Sanchez	Co-Founder Mojo Global
Craig Shelley	COO of Impact Realty
Cynthia Kersey	Founder of Unstoppable Foundation
Danny Creed	Hall of Fame Business Coach
Danny Savage	CEO of Mortgage Coach
David Baer	Creative Partner at The Prepared Group
David Fagan	CEO of Icon Builder Media
Debbie Allen	Best-Selling Author of Highly Paid Experts
Dennis Doran	Author of Soft as Steel
Earl Kemper	CEO of The Premier Dentistry Advisory Group
Elias Zepeda	CEO of Need Clients NOW
Emily Letran	High Performance Dental Coach
Emmeline Saavedra	President of The Champions Institute
Eric Lofholm	CEO of Eric Lofholm International
Gail Watson	CEO of Women Speakers Association
Gelie Akhenblit	President of Gelie Media
Harrison Rogers	CEO of HJR Global
Itamar Shafir	CEO of Umbrella Micro Enterprises Int.
Ivan Misner	Founder of BNI Business Network
James Miller	CEO of Network After Work
Jay Fiset	Founder & CEO of JVology
Jeff Hoffman	Chairman of Global Entrepreneurship Network
Jeffrey Hayzlett	CEO of C-Suite Network
Jerry Conti	CEO of BoomSTR & LuxHomePro
Jesse Doubek	CEO of Influencer Technologies

Jill Lublin	PR Guru
Jim Canfield	President of CEO Tools
John Jantsch	Best-Selling Author of Duct Tape Marketing
Julienne O'Connor	High Performance Dental Coach
Kim Marie Branch-Pettid	CEO of LeTip
Kristine Vowles	CEO of The Luxury Look
Kyle Fuller	CEO of Factum Financial
Dr. Len Tau DMD	Founder of Raving Patients
Lisa Patrick	Founder of Thought Leaders Roundtable
Lynn Rose	CEO of WowMaker
Mark Victor Hansen	World's #1 Best-Selling Non-Fiction Author
Michela Quilici	Co-Founder of Global Business Connectors
Mike Keeter	Business Development Expert Nobel Biocare
Noah St. John	Founder of Success Clinic
Omar Sayed	CEO of Sperse
Pamela Stambaugh	President & Founder of Accountability Pays
Preston Weekes	Chief Strategy Officer of Operations X
Renee Piane	World Renowned Dating Expert
Robert W. Jones	CEO of iNetrepreneur Network
Shea Vaughn	Founder of WWTVN Worldwide TV Network
Steve Farber	CEO of The Extreme Leadership Network
Steve Rodgers	Spiritual Business Activist
Stuart Gethner	CEO of Gethner Education & Consulting
Thomas Evans	President of HOA.com
Tisha Pelletier	Personal Branding Expert
Todd Bookspan	Creator of Win by Noon
Tom Crawford	Managing Principal of Telehealth Partners
Tom Gay	CEO of TribeUp
Dr. Tony Allessandro	Founder of Assessments 24 x 7

Scan the QR code below or use this link to view a video message about the impact this book can deliver to your business and beyond. Share with your social sphere to give them some great content they will love.

https://ravingreferrals.com/imagine/

IMAGINE...

Have you ever wanted to make a more significant difference in the world?

Now don't just skip past this question. Take a moment to give it some thought.

What would you do if your business was so successful that you suddenly found yourself with all the fortune and fame you've always dreamed of?

What if you had flocks of perfect prospects and ideal clients flooding to your business because of your stellar reputation and superb service?

What if you were a recognized expert and respected authority in your field?

What if other businesses paid you to travel the world sharing your knowledge and wisdom with their employees, partners, and clients?

How would you use your newfound influence and affluence? Would you simply retire and live out your days on some golf course or sunny beach? Or would you use your wealth and wisdom for good?

WE'RE ON A MISSION

We're asking you these questions because we're on a mission to impact and empower every person on the planet.

You see, we believe every man, woman, and child deserves nutritious food, clean water, exceptional healthcare, empowering education, and opportunities for financial freedom.

Now, you may think the possibility of achieving that goal is entirely unrealistic, and you might just be right. But the one thing we know is that every time we share our purpose and vision with others, we experience a deep sense of fulfillment and satisfaction. And we're willing to bet you feel that same indescribable joy every time you make a meaningful difference in the lives of others.

As you read this book, mastering the strategies that unlock all the income and influence you desire and deserve, we hope that you will, in turn, positively impact and uplift your clients, customers, co-workers, employees, vendors, and referral partners as well as your friends, family, neighbors, and community.

Together, we can make a difference and change the world in meaningful ways.

Brandon

Table of Contents

Preface xxi

Introduction xxxi

1. What's Your Referral Score? 1
2. The 7 Laws of Raving Referrals 13
3. Perfect Prospects & Lifetime Clients 25
4. Learn Why They Buy 35
5. Establish Your Expert Status 43
6. Engage Your Referral Champions 55
7. Create a Raving Rewards Program 73
8. Master the Art of the Ask 87
9. Client Appreciation Events 97
10. Referral of a Lifetime 103
11. Wealth Through Workshops 111
12. Partner with Top Trusted Pros 117
13. Network Strategically 129
14. Create Your Referral Alliance 139
15. Leverage LinkedIn 149

16. The Referral Partner Blueprint 163
17. Top 21 Cross Promotion Campaigns 171
Time For ACTION 207
Success Scripts 209
Experts & Influencers 217
National Networking Organizations & Resources 251
Become A Raving Referrals Co-Author 263
Become A Raving Referrals Certified Trainer 265
About The Author 267

Preface

CONGRATULATIONS!

For Investing in Yourself and Your Business
For Pursuing a Faster Path to Success
For Discovering the System to Raving Referrals

Since you're reading this book, we know a few things about you...

1. Your business may not be quite where you want it to be. You simply aren't getting the kind of leads, referrals, prospects, and clients you need to earn the income you want.
2. Most likely, you are skilled at providing your service and just need a better system when it comes to marketing and business development.
3. Perhaps you feel awkward and uncomfortable asking for referrals, so you don't receive them as consistently as you'd like.
4. You already know some of the principles and practices in this book. Still, you don't have a formalized referral system and sometimes rely on divine intervention, hoping new client opportunities will appear each week.

5. Most importantly, you are serious about changing all that, and you're looking for a system that will generate a steady stream of highly qualified and profitable prospects.

You Are On The Right Path!

This book will empower you with time-tested, proven strategies, scripts, and secrets obtained from over two decades of researching, refining, and perfecting the referral process.

What we can give you goes far beyond simple theory. We've used these powerful principles and practices to build what we believe is the single most comprehensive and effective referral marketing system the world has ever known.

We are passionately committed to helping you transform your business to create a consistent and dependable flow of *Raving Referrals* and profitable prospects that turn into lifetime clients.

Our goal is that you start each week with a calendar that is full of new client appointments, so you never have to worry about where your next referral is coming from. Imagine meeting with people every day who already trust you because they've been referred by a loyal friend or professional that they have known for years.

I say "we" because WE IS THE KEY. This book is all about changing your mindset and approach when it comes to growing your business. Rather than being a lone wolf always out hunting for new opportunities by yourself, we want you to have a tribe of talented and trusted people you work with who are constantly helping refer clients back and forth so everyone wins together.

As you apply the Raving Referrals process, perfect prospects will flock to you, gift wrapped with trust, respect, and ready for the solutions and services you provide.

The Results Are In

Most business owners and professionals understand and agree that referrals are the best source of new business. After all, decades of research have proven this time and time again.

Empirical studies from major universities, publications, and research firms have concluded:

- People are 400% more likely to buy from you when they are referred.
- 90% of people trust recommendations from people they know.
- Referred clients are 16% more profitable than non-referred clients.
- 84% of Business-To-Business (B2B) sales start with a referral

So, if referrals are so profitable, why do so many professionals struggle to develop a personal practice that generates new client opportunities consistently?

What Holds You Back?

If you're like most of the professionals we serve, you may fall into one of the following categories:

- You're just too busy staying busy.
- You're new to your job, industry, or area and are just getting your business started.
- You don't seem to know the right people or have a strong enough network yet.
- You've never learned to build your business by referral,and you aren't really sure how to start.

If any of these things have held you back in the past, you may feel like you grind away, day after day, making tedious cold calls, buying bad leads, or throwing away good money on poorly performing marketing campaigns.

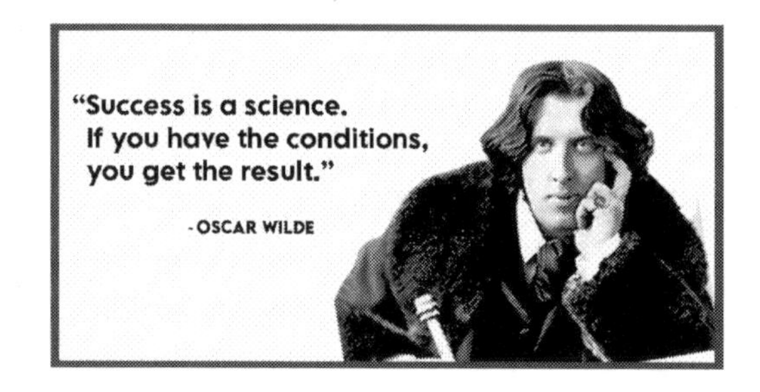

Perhaps you've been studying referrals for years and even belong to a BNI, LeTip, chamber of commerce, or local leads group. You may already be getting some referrals and are looking to expand and improve the quantity and quality of the referrals you receive.

The good news is that if you simply follow the step-by-step process explained in this book, you can systematically build a strong referral business that will generate referrals for years to come.

Stop the Insanity

You've heard the definition of insanity is to do the same thing over and over and expect different results. Well, we want to commend you for investing in yourself and taking the time to learn these time-tested and proven referral tactics instead of just doing what you've always done.

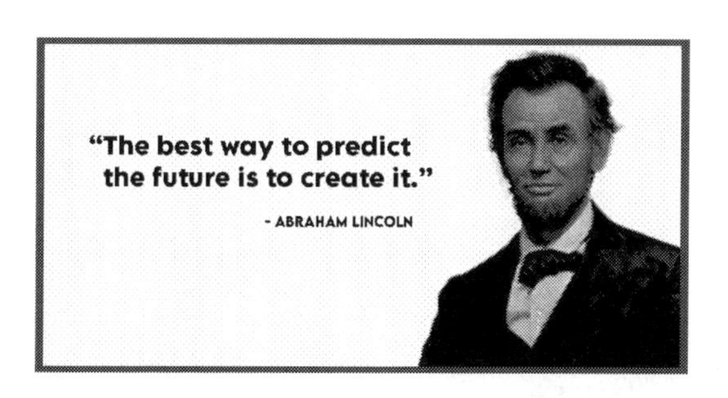

What we're going to teach you will be a total game-changer for you, your business, and your family... but only if you take action and implement the simple steps outlined in this book.

After all, ACTION is the key to activating the law of attrACTION.

If you follow this proven program and consistently take the quick and easy success steps we will guide you through, your business and bank account will grow. As you expand your income, you'll unlock financial freedom and the time freedom you desire and deserve.

Our goal is to help you attract *Raving Referrals* quickly and consistently so you can spend more time doing what you love with the people you love. Whether pursuing your passions and hobbies, serving in your favorite charity or church, or traveling the world enjoying amazing experiences, everything you want can be achieved once you learn the secrets and the science of attracting *Raving Referrals*.

So that's our vision for you. But what's your goal?

How Much Money Do You Want to Make?

Ultimately, the number one reason you are reading this book is that you want to earn more money. If that's true for you, it's imperative that you set an attainable goal for exactly how much you want to earn over the next 12 months. You can then use your financial target as motivation to stay on track and take the actions needed to achieve your goal.

What is your Annual Income Goal for the next 12 months?

$ ______________________

What's Your WHY?

Now that you've declared how much money you want to earn in the next year, let's explore what really drives you. The following questions will help you gain clarity on your true reasons for achieving your Annual Income Goal.

1. Why is it important to you to increase your income and achieve your financial goal?

I want to belief I can have a successful profitable coaching business

2. What would achieving your financial goal allow you to do that you can't do right now?

Feel more relaxed & productive about my business. Less anxious/feel about marketing

3. How will people benefit when you reach your goal?
   - Your Family (spouse, children, and grandchildren) - ease of my pocket
   - Your Friends
   - Your Company - Confident
   - Your Employees
   - Your Favorite Charities - Vision

4. How will your friends and family feel about you when you achieve your goal? ?

5. Beyond the money, how will you feel about yourself once you have achieved this level of financial success?

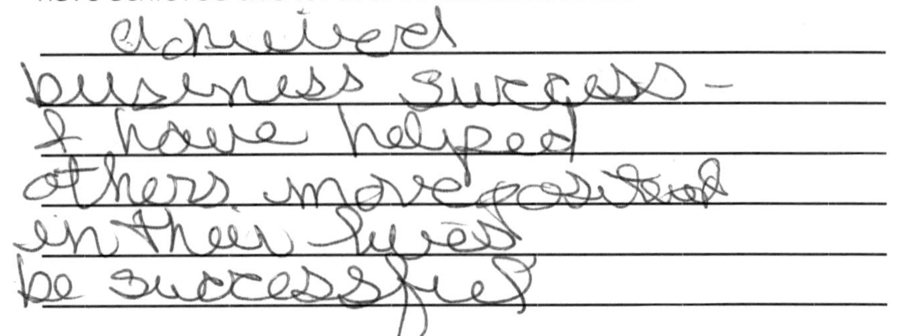

The reason it's so important to understand your *WHY* is that it is your *WHY* that really drives us as human beings. The clearer you are about *WHY* you want to achieve your desired outcome, the more driven and committed you will be to create those results.

Enlist Others in Your Success

To achieve success faster, share your goal with others who can help you reach it. This might include a business coach, partner, manager, employees, or even your referral partners. Ask them to hold you accountable or even partner on the program so they can build their business as you build yours.

After all, if you really want to lose weight, hiring a personal trainer committed to your success will dramatically increase your results. Just having a membership to the gym doesn't mean you actually show up and work out. Having a personal trainer that will hold you accountable ensures that when it comes to working out, you are doing what you should, when you should, exactly how you should. Granted, it takes time to see the results, but you will feel stronger, faster, and fitter over time. You'll see old fat transform into new muscle. You'll start to notice new lines and indentations on your stomach and problem areas where before there were only bulges and curves.

When it comes to building your business, the reality is you want as many people as possible invested in your success and cheering you on. The more champions you have for your business, the more business you will have.

From Success to Significance

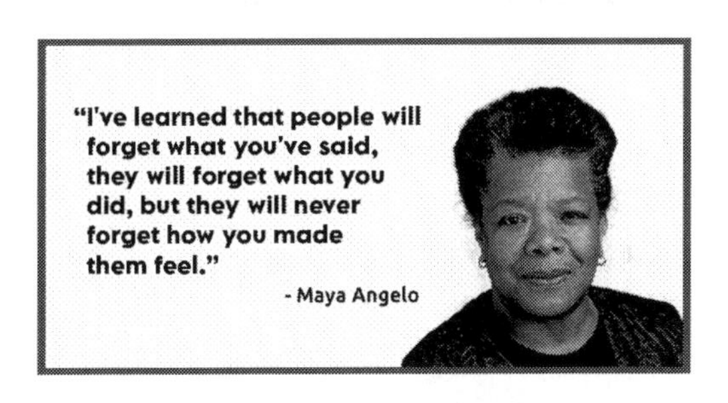

What's exciting to realize is that the success you create throughout your life and career can impact future generations if you do it right. Not just for you and your spouse. When you achieve serious success, you can leave a lasting legacy that changes the lives of your children, your grandchildren, and generations to come. Not to mention the impact you can have on your community and the causes you care about.

Our mission is to transform the lives of business professionals around the world. That's why we are so committed to empowering and equipping you with the knowledge and tools that you need to succeed.

We want you to feel so confident and comfortable that you will take action immediately and that you'll consistently apply what we're going to teach you. If you do, you WILL get more referrals and clients, guaranteed!

We love what we do because we get to work with some of the best people and companies on the planet. There's nothing more rewarding than hearing stories of professionals worldwide who have gained financial freedom as a result of our system.

Our request is that as you put these practices and principles to work in your business, you will share your wins and success stories with us at **RavingReferrals.com/success**. We'd love nothing more than to spotlight your victories with our growing global community of people who are living a life powered by *Raving Referrals.*

Ready for us to show you the money? Scan the QR code below or use this link for a quick video message from Brandon Barnum:

https://ravingreferrals.com/money

Introduction

Getting Personal

Over the past 27 years, I have been blessed to be mentored by some of the world's most influential and affluent people. My career and professional travels have led me around the world to exciting locations, including Hong Kong, Macau, and Beijing, China; London, England; Zurich, Switzerland; Rome, Italy; Athens, Greece; Bogotá, Colombia; Caracas, Venezuela; Freetown, Sierra Leone; and Accra, Ghana.

I've hiked the Great Wall of China, convened in the U.S. Supreme Court in Washington D.C., celebrated with the 2nd man to walk on the moon, and flew in a private plane over Angel Falls, the tallest waterfall in the world smack dab in the Amazon rainforest.

I've been involved in billions of dollars of transactions, met with CEOs of massive corporations including Prudential, Patron, Paul Mitchell, Blockbuster, and Bank of America. I've hired top executives to help build my brands and grow my businesses, including the former Chief Marketing Officer from Mastercard and the former CEO of Guerilla Marketing.

I've taught countless people around the world through seminars, conferences, and webinars and have been blessed to have some of the world's most amazing thought leaders teaching our students. Authors and luminaries like Mark

Victor Hansen of *Chicken Soup for the Soul,* Jack Canfield of *The Success Principles*, Michael Beckwith from *The Secret*, John Gray of *Men Are from Mars, Women Are From Venus*, Brendon Burchard of *High Performing Habits*, Chris and Janet Attwood of *The Passion Test*, and visionary futurists including Barbara Marx Hubbard, Dr. Don Beck, Lynn Twist, and Dr. Jean Houston to name a few, have been faculty members teaching and training our clients and community.

I've raised and donated millions of dollars for great charities, both here and abroad. One of my favorite projects was helping design and execute a fundraising campaign for the Mineseeker Foundation, whose patrons included Richard Branson, Brad Pitt, Queen Noor of Jordan, and Nelson Mandella, all of whom banded together to eliminate landmines from the face of the planet.

I've met with African chiefs, operated a diamond mine on the Gold Coast of Africa, and produced the single largest training of teachers in the African nation of Liberia presided over by the President of Liberia herself.

I was even fortunate enough to meet my idol and personal hero – Bono, the lead singer of the band U2.

Needless to say, at the age of 51, I've lived a rich, exciting, and fulfilling life.

The reason I share all of this with you is not to impress you but to impress upon you that anything you dream and desire is possible. Every single one of the incidents and relationships I mentioned came after an introduction or referral.

Before I teach you how to attract all the clients, customers, partners, and people you need to fulfill your purpose and passions, let me take you back to the beginning of my story.

Humble Beginnings

As a child from a divorced home in the 1970s, my hippy mom hopped from job to job, never caring much about money or financial stability. Her wanderlust led to constant moves, which meant I had to attend different schools each and every year from kindergarten through sixth grade.

In addition to constantly changing where we lived, my mom was also continually changing jobs and careers. She did everything from working as a mechanic for Southern Pacific Railroad, working retail for a thrift shop, selling insurance, and even operating a bakery before eventually selling real estate.

Money was tight, and I grew up with vivid memories of watching Mom buy groceries with government food stamps. Then I would go to school, where they were nice enough to give me tickets for free breakfast and free lunch every day to ensure I had food to eat and didn't go hungry.

As you might imagine, after living with so little growing up, my true hunger was for success, so I grew up eager to achieve wealth and prosperity as far back as I can remember.

My First Referral Experience

My first experience with referrals came back in 1985 when I signed up for the Columbia House record and tape club. I was so excited to get my first shipment of 13 cassette tapes, which arrived for the low cost of just one penny (plus shipping and handling, of course).

This was the 80's, so I had all the popular albums by bands like U2, The Jacksons, Duran Duran, Thompson Twins, Journey, and many more. What excited me most was their offer to send me four more cassette tapes for each person I signed up for the music membership.

I quickly got 12 other kids from my high school to pay their penny and sign up for the program. It wasn't long before 48 more albums arrived. For a poor teenager with little money, it felt like I had won the lottery! My friends marveled at my music collection, and I enjoyed having albums from obscure artists like Icicle Works and Flock of Seagulls. You've gotta love the 80's.

That experience taught me the power that generating referrals can have on a business. It was also the first example I'd seen of a Referral Rewards program. Since then, I've used that same strategy to personally generate over $500,000,000 in closed transactions by referral.

Single Dad Life

My professional career started a decade later. I was 25 years old, still fresh out of college, and working as the Marketing Director for a regional estate planning law firm.

Having recently been awarded custody of my 2-year-old son, Sebastian, I found myself as a young single dad faced with many new life challenges, the biggest being financial.

With outrageous daycare expenses piled on top of my mortgage, I soon found myself faced with too much month at the end of the money. Can you relate?

After bouncing mortgage checks multiple times, I knew I had to change my financial situation if I was ever going to provide for my son. After exploring various opportunities and industries, I decided to accept a mortgage loan officer position at a prominent Savings and Loan. That's where I first uncovered the art and science of attracting *Raving Referrals*.

Mentored to Millions

As I started my new job, I was desperate to build my book of business. I felt intimidated, having no experience, no network, and no clue how to get either one. Needless to say, those first few months were rough!

As fortune would have it, one of my state's top producing loan officers worked at the desk next to mine. Every day I studied by his side, soaking up everything I could learn from this top producer who earned hundreds of thousands of dollars each year.

What amazed me is that this man had absolutely no personality. In fact, the rest of the office would giggle as he answered his phone, stating his name with a droll monotone that sounded like it belonged to the teacher from *Ferris Bueller's Day Off*: "Anyone? Anyone?"

Despite his lack of charisma, this man's phone rang off the hook with new loan applications. He was earning tens of thousands of dollars in commissions each month working 9 am to 5 pm and was generating the level of income and success I was hungry for.

So, I watched and listened in awe, asking as many questions as possible to learn his secrets for attracting so much business. I *had* to know what he was doing that made him so super successful.

It turns out he had cracked the code on attracting referrals. Over the years, he had built relationships with top professionals in complementary industries who were already serving the clients he wanted to attract. These pros were happy to refer clients to him because he had earned their trust and respect.

As a result, he never had to spend a dime on marketing and rarely spent any time prospecting. He had all the clients he could comfortably manage and rarely had to leave his desk except to grab some coffee and collect his fat paychecks.

As I studied this man's business intensively, I interviewed other top-producing mortgage and real estate professionals because I was committed to learning how the top 10% consistently outperformed the bottom 90% by leaps and bounds.

Lessons from Top Producers

These top producers taught me how the super successful generate massive income consistently and almost effortlessly. I learned proven tips, scripts, and strategies that have opened doors I could never have entered on my own.

By consistently engaging complementary professionals, I built deep, meaningful, trust-filled relationships that gave me referrals which helped 10X my income from $20,000 to over $200,000 annually in just 18 months after entering the mortgage business.

Since that time, I've used this formula to build relationships with some of the world's most affluent and influential people who have graciously recommended me to their clients and colleagues.

Needless to say, referrals have changed my life and continue to drive my success now over twenty years later. It's been an amazing adventure so far, and I hope you'll join me on this ride.

Since those early days, I helped build the world's largest referral network with more than five million members in over 200 countries. Now, as Chairman and CEO of HOA.com, I spend my time training and empowering the next generation of professionals and small business owners to grow their businesses by referral: challenging and empowering them to do more, be more, earn more, and give more for the betterment of all.

My hope is that you too will master these keys to *Raving Referrals* and that they forever change your life. If you implement just one of these success steps each week, you can increase your referral

business and attract all the income, impact, and influence you desire and deserve.

What Will Your Story Be?

We want to help you massively transform your business and your life so that you have a compelling success story we can share with the world.

We hope you find so much value in our book and our *Referral Marketing System* that you too will share your story and our solution with others. After all, your story can inspire and motivate others to follow your steps and achieve the same results and success that you will have achieved.

We've combined all of the proven best practices in both marketing and referral generation into one fast, easy to use, and proven Referral Marketing System that will help you do three things:

1. Engage Your Referral Champions
2. Partner with Trusted Professionals
3. Promote Yourself and Your Team

Taking these three actions consistently will help you achieve top of mind awareness with your clients and social sphere that will generate referrals consistently. After all, your existing contacts and network already know hundreds, if not thousands, of people who fit your perfect prospect profile.

That's why we are going to teach you how to promote yourself and your services in a way that makes people view you as *THE* trusted solution they've been looking for to solve the challenges they face.

We'll teach you how to team up and partner with top professionals who already serve your ideal clients. Your strategic alliances will promote you to their best clients, colleagues, and social sphere as you follow our proven process.

Finally, our system will help you engage your relationships strategically to build instant rapport and deep trust. This will lead clients to do more business with you and ultimately refer you to their family, friends, co-workers, and colleagues, giving you all of the business, you could ever want.

First, let's assess your current *Referral Score* so you can see the progress you make once you put these *Raving Referrals* practices to work.

Scan the QR code below or use this link for a special message about growing your business by 10X over the next 1-2 years: https://ravingreferrals.com/first

CHAPTER 1

What's Your Referral Score?

As you begin your journey towards achieving your Annual Income Goal, it's crucial to understand precisely where you are starting from and what gaps you might have in your current referral business practices.

If you study the top performers and producers in your industry, you'll likely find that they all exhibit the same daily practices. By making a few minor changes to your daily habits, you can reach the same level of financial success that the top performers in your company and industry have achieved.

We've developed a *Referral Score* assessment to help you understand how well you're currently performing in each of the ten daily practices that drive referrals.

This tool has been designed to identify quick and easy improvements to your business processes that can drive referrals for years to come.

Let's look specifically at the top ten actions that drive referrals and see how you measure up. As you review each practice, write down your self-assessed score on each of these daily practices. This will give you your baseline *Referral Score* and identify simple yet powerful opportunities for improvement.

Before you read on, scan this QR code or use this link below for a special message about the **Raving Referrals Referral Score Quiz:**

https://ravingreferrals.com/quiz/

#1 PLANNING YOUR SUCCESS

Every successful business owner has a detailed business plan for how they will achieve their goals and objectives. However, when it comes to referrals, this doesn't often hold true.

We're amazed how few professionals actually have a written plan that details exactly what they are going to do this week, this month, and this year to grow their referral business.

Considering the fact that over 65% of new business comes by referral, you are leaving money on the table if you don't have a written plan and system to drive referrals for your business.

Your plan should include your goals for the month, quarter, and year along with a detailed promotional plan and communication calendar, so you plan out your key offers and campaigns throughout the year.

How do you score when it comes to having a detailed business development and referral plan?

Rate yourself on a scale of 0-10, where 0 indicates you have no plan at all and 10 means you have a detailed action plan with written goals, promotions, and a communication calendar.

1. Planning 2

#2 SERVING YOUR CLIENTS

When it comes to business, nothing matters more than serving your clients!

Providing exceptional service to each and every client, customer, patient, guest, and community member should be the reason you do what you do. The money is simply the reward for a job well done!

The more exceptionally you serve your clients, the more referrals will flow your way. As people see how much you care about their success and satisfaction, they will naturally be more inclined to refer others to you.

On a scale of 0-10, how well do you score when it comes to serving your clients? Write down your score to practice #2 now.

2. Serving ______________

#3 ENGAGING PEOPLE CONSISTENTLY

The most successful professionals ensure they engage and connect with their most important relationships consistently.

As you invest time and energy in building strong relationships, you increase the number of people who know, like, and trust you enough to refer you to the people in their lives. The key is to engage them consistently while focusing on the things that matter most TO THEM.

After all, people don't care how much you know until they know how much you care. The more consistently you engage others personally and meaningfully, the more consistently they will recommend and refer you to their friends, family, colleagues, and social sphere.

So how do you score when it comes to connecting with and engaging people? Are you skillful at following up and building strong relationships, or do people rarely hear from you after they've met you for the first time?

Write down your score, with 0 being awful and 10 being masterful.

3. Engaging 4

#4 ASKING FOR REFERRALS

We're often amazed how few professionals actually ask their clients for referrals. Most people in business understand that referrals drive their success, but often they feel awkward and uncomfortable asking for them. That's probably because they've never been taught when and how to ask for referrals in a way that makes your clients feel comfortable and happy to help.

We are going to teach you to master "The Art of the Ask" in Chapter 8. For now, be sure to write down your score of how consistent you are at asking for referrals from both your clients and professional colleagues.

4. Asking 4

#5 TRACKING YOUR REFERRALS

The most successful professionals always measure and track their results, especially when it comes to referrals!

We're surprised how few people actually understand where their business comes from. After all, if you aren't tracking and measuring where each and every client comes from, how can you expect to maximize your results?

Business experts teach, "What gets measured, gets maximized," and that is absolutely true. By tracking your referrals, you focus your mind on the #1 driver of your business success. The information you gather allows you to concentrate your valuable time and energy on your most productive and profitable relationships.

Okay, it's time to score how good you are at tracking the referrals you give and receive. Go ahead and write down your score now.

5. Tracking 2

#6 THANKING PEOPLE WHO GIVE REFERRALS

Thanking people is a critical practice that can dramatically impact your success... if you do it consistently. Every time you receive a referral, you should be thanking the person who made the recommendation or introduction. Not only does this help them feel good because you've recognized them, but it also demonstrates your professionalism, which reinforces their feeling that recommending you was the right move to make.

Thanking referrers will dramatically boost their confidence in recommending you and improve the probability they send you more referrals in the future.

Please understand, this is one of the fastest and easiest ways to grow your referral business, so make sure you thank people each and every time they give you a new referral.

So how do you rate when it comes to consistently thanking people who give you referrals?

6. Thanking 5

#7 UPDATING PEOPLE WHO GIVE REFERRALS

Updating people who give you referrals is another important practice that builds trust. People are highly appreciative when you call, text, DM, or email a quick update, letting them know if you were able to help their client, friend, or loved one.

This is especially true when the person giving you the referral is another professional. After all, they've entrusted their own personal credibility and relationship with their client to you. Following up with a quick update gives you a natural and comfortable opportunity to ask if they know anyone else who would benefit from your service.

If you've never even thought about updating people after they refer people to you, you may need to write down a score of 0 on this practice. On the other hand, maybe you are awesome at letting people know what's going on with the people they refer to you. If so, then write down a 10. Just be sure to write down your number so you can see your overall Referral Score.

7. Updating 9

#8 REWARDING PEOPLE WHO GIVE REFERRALS

Rewarding your referral sources is another excellent business practice and catalyst for referrals, whether you incentivize people or simply surprise them with a gift when they refer you.

Some professionals design and promote a formal *Raving Rewards* program where clients and promotional partners are incentivized through cash, prizes, or free services when they introduce prospects or customers to your business.

We love *Raving Rewards* programs because they help create a culture of referrals. Plus, when designed properly, these programs automatically ask for referrals on your behalf without you ever having to leave your comfort zone.

On the other hand, simply surprising people with a gift card for coffee, the movies, or a nice local restaurant is a generous gesture people will not soon forget.

Just be sure to research and follow the regulations and restrictions for your industry, so you are always in complete compliance.

So how good you are at rewarding people who give you referrals. Are you a 0, a 10, or somewhere in between?

8. Rewarding 4

#9 RECOGNIZING PEOPLE WHO GIVE REFERRALS

Most people love to be publicly recognized for doing good work and helping others. In fact, our frail human ego has a very strong desire and need for recognition, especially in today's social media obsessed world of likes, shares, tweets, and follows.

That's why many businesses grow rapidly once they start publicly celebrating and recognizing people who promote and refer them. Whether it be in the public areas of the business or through a newsletter, website or social media accounts, the social proof and credibility built by recognizing your referrers works quickly and effectively.

How about you? How well do you score when it comes to celebrating and recognizing the people who recommend and refer you? Write down your score so we can move to the final referral practice that drives your wealth.

9. Recognizing 3

#10 PROMOTING YOURSELF AND YOUR SERVICES

Nearly 90% of business success comes down to your marketing and lead generation. After all, if you have enough sales and revenue coming in the door, most other problems can be solved. On the other hand, if you don't have a consistent flow of new clients, leads, and sales opportunities for your business, you don't really have much of a business, do you?

After coaching, consulting, and working with thousands of businesses worldwide, we've found where most people fail is in their self-promotion and marketing efforts. Rather than attending events, networking, mailing out offers, or running ads online and off, many people simply do unprofitable "busy-work" that never gets them any closer to their Annual Income Goal. Whether that be because they are too busy, too shy, or just don't know-how, they simply don't invest enough time or money attracting new business opportunities.

How do you rate yourself in the marketing and promotion side of your business?

If you are one of those people who always find a reason not to invest your time or money promoting yourself and your services, you may need to give yourself a 1, 2, or 3 on this practice. If you are a super promoter who always stays top-of-mind with your clients, customers, fans, and followers, you should write down a 9 or a 10. Most people score between 3 and 5 on this one, so don't feel bad if you didn't score well on this important practice.

10. Promoting 3

TIME FOR THE TALLY

Now for the fun part! Write down and add up each of your scores from the 10 referral best practices above.

1. Planning 2
2. Serving 9
3. Engaging 4
4. Asking 4

5. Tracking	2
6. Thanking	5
7. Updating	9
8. Rewarding	4
9. Recognizing	3
10. Promoting	3
TOTAL REFERRAL SCORE	45

Your Referral Score ranges from 0-100 and works just like a standard school grade. That means...

If you scored 90 or higher, you get an A

We'll bet you dollars to doughnuts that you are in the top 5% of income earners in your company and industry. You're probably already earning a great 6-figure income and living the good life. You have solid systems in place that generate referrals consistently and automatically. Most likely, you take multiple vacations each year and share your abundance with everyone you love.

We hope every single one of our readers achieves this level of Referral Score after going through the training in this book and setting up your Referral Marketing System.

If you scored in this range, we congratulate and celebrate you. Well done!

If you scored between 80-89, you get a B

Most people who score this high are in the top 20% of income earners in their industry and company. You likely have new referrals and opportunities coming to you on a daily basis and are doing quite well financially.

If you got a B on this test, you should feel proud for mastering so many of the referral best practices. Business must be pretty good, and your income is increasing. You're on your way, and it's just a matter of time before you blast through your Annual Income Goal.

If you scored between 70-79, your grade is a C

In the Olympics, third place still gets you on the podium, so feel proud of what you've accomplished thus far. Just know there's more work to do to reach gold medal status.

This is still a passing mark. You are likely in the top half of the producers in your firm or industry and are doing fine financially. You may have identified some opportunities for improvement as you reviewed these top 10 practices. Hopefully, you are now motivated to learn and apply the proven strategies, systems, and scripts we share in this book.

If you scored between 60-69, that means you got a D

If you're in this category, you're not alone. The majority of professionals initially get a failing *Referral Score* before they go through our program and apply our strategies. The knowledge and wisdom in this book can help you identify quick tweaks that help ramp up your revenue and maximize profitability.

If you are serious about growing your business and generating more income, just work on each of these daily practices and take consistent action. Fortunately, our easy-to-use system can help boost your score significantly.

If you scored below 60, you know what grade you got...

The optimists in us would tell you that scoring in this range just means you have many opportunities for improvement. Remember, this isn't your final grade. It's just the beginning. There is a lot you can do to quickly boost your *Referral Score* and your income.

The power behind building a business by referral is that you actually compound your success once you start because more new clients refer more new clients who refer more new clients.

We're Here to Help

If you're feeling a bit stretched, stressed, or overwhelmed right now, we totally understand. Don't worry! We are committed to teaching you all you need to know to build a thriving business.

You'll be retaking this test at the end of this book, so just focus on putting these practices to work in your business, and you'll see your referrals and income start to rise.

If you haven't already taken your
Referral Score Quiz online, scan this QR code
or visit the link below to take the quick quiz now.

https://ravingreferrals.com/quiz/

CHAPTER 2

The 7 Laws of Raving Referrals

When it comes to generating *Raving Referrals* for your business, there are seven laws you need to understand and master. When you build your business in accordance with these seven laws, you will attract a steady stream of new client opportunities for years to come.

Raving Referral Law #1:

Every Referral Starts with Trust

The first thing you must understand when it comes to referrals is that every referral starts with trust.

Think about the last referral, recommendation, or introduction you gave to a friend, client, or colleague. How well did you know and trust the person you recommended?

Most likely, you trust them tremendously, or you would not have made that recommendation, right? If not, you gave the recommendation with a disclaimer saying something like, "I've never used them myself, but I hear they do a good job."

The same is true for everyone you know. The more they know, like, and ultimately trust you, the more they will sing your praises and passionately endorse you to the people in their lives.

In fact, your income is directly tied to the amount of trust that you build with your clients, colleagues, and social sphere. The more trust you earn, the more money you will earn over your career.

Gallup has conducted polls over the past several decades that consistently show that the most trusted professions on the planet are also the most highly paid, including doctors, engineers, and accountants.

The more people that trust that you are a person of integrity and an expert professional in your trade, the more confidence they will have in recommending you. Ultimately it is their trust in you that gives them the confidence to refer people they care about to you and your business.

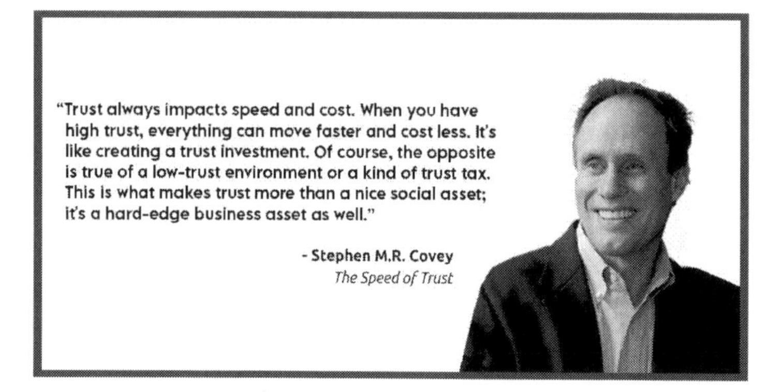

Raving Referral Law #2:

The More You Give, The More You Receive

Giving is the key that builds trust, deepens relationships, and unlocks referrals. The Bible teaches, "*As you sow, so shall you reap.*" That timeless truth definitely applies to your referral business.

The more generous you are with your time, attention, understanding, and respect for others, the more liked and trusted you will become. In turn, people will go out of their way to help you succeed.

In life, there are people who take more than they give and those who give more than they take. Those who are constantly putting their own wants and needs first are typically viewed as selfish, egotistical, and greedy. Those who give generously tend to be viewed as noble, big-hearted, and even charitable.

So which camp do you want to be in?

Take a moment to think about the people in your life who are the greatest givers. Who are the three people you view as being most generous and giving of your family, friends, colleagues, and co-workers?

The 3 Most Generous People in My Life Are:

1. ______________________________
2. ______________________________
3. ______________________________

How do you FEEL about the people you just identified? Does their generosity make you like them more?

Most likely, the answer is a resounding *YES!*

That's why when it comes to building trust, the more you give, the more you receive. Make it your mission to go out of your way to give your time, talents, attention, and best efforts in all you do.

Give your respect and attention to everyone you meet. Listen to them intently and ask probing questions about their passions and pursuits. Get to know what they really care about and help them achieve it if you can.

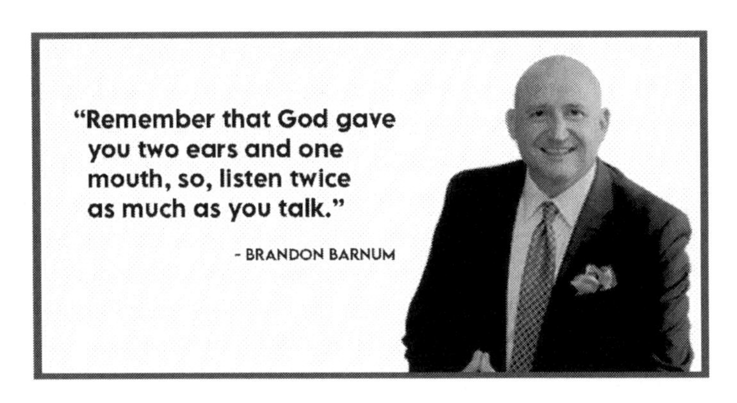

Give praise and public appreciation when people help you. Post a quick shout-out on social media or send them a thank you card, text, or testimonial for their business.

The more you give, the more referrals you will receive. So give generously in all you do.

Raving Referral Law #3:

Relationships Trigger Transactions

You've probably heard the saying that people don't care how much you know until they know how much you care. As you build trust and give generously, you will strengthen and deepen relationships with people who have the ability to refer and recommend all the clients you will ever want or need.

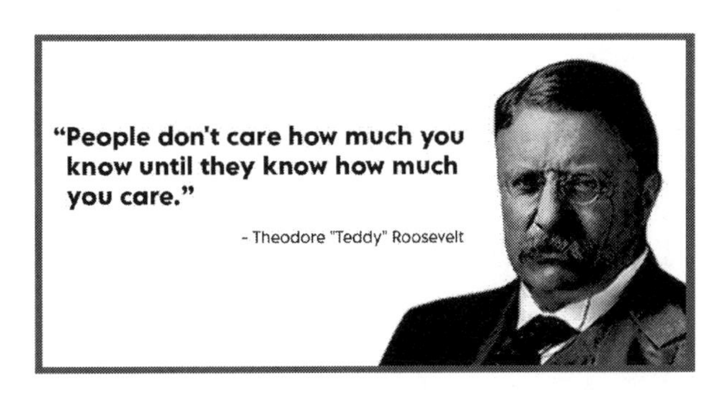

The reality is that trust only gets built through relationships. This is why the third law of Raving Referrals is that relationships trigger transactions.

The quality of your relationships determines the quality of your life.

Before getting married, my wife and I went through a premarital course with the pastor of our church. One of the lessons he taught us was that relationships were like bank accounts. Every time you show someone you care about them, you make a deposit in that account, and your balance with them grows.

The more often you connect with the people in your life, the greater your relational equity with them will be. The better they get to know you, the more they start to like you and trust you, which then leads to them recommending and referring you and your firm.

It makes sense, doesn't it?

Most banks charge service fees on inactive accounts, and the same thing happens with your relationships. The more time you let pass without communicating or connecting, your relational balance with that person declines.

If you don't reach out from time to time, they may actually forget about you altogether. They certainly won't be on the lookout for clients for you, which is what you want for your business.

That is why it's so important to continually engage and nurture all your Referral Champions, including your clients, referral partners, and social sphere.

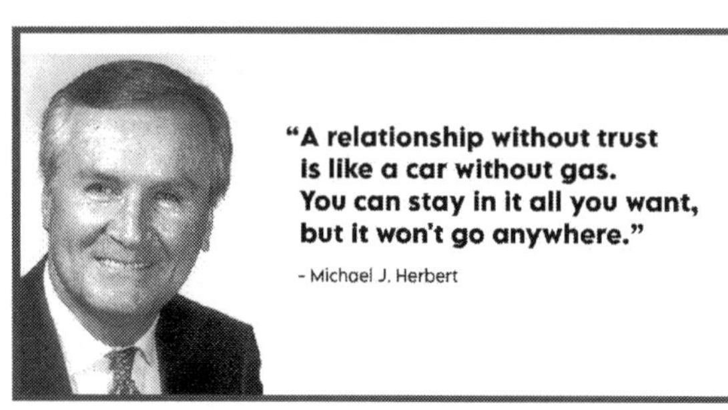

Of course, it's always best to connect with people live in person, because humans experience the strongest bonds when we are hanging out together having fun. That's why we recommend that you get together with your top relationships at least once every month or two.

That said, you can always send a text, call them on the phone, or send a personal message or handwritten note to show you are thinking about them. When you do, you are making relational deposits that will pay off big time once you learn the secrets to generating referrals.

The more personal your interactions are, the more relational equity you are creating. Remember that every touch counts. Even a quick text, email, direct message, social post, or newsletter will help you gain mindshare. Just remind your referral champions you are never too busy to help them and the people they care about. The more value you deliver to your relationships, the more frequently they will refer you.

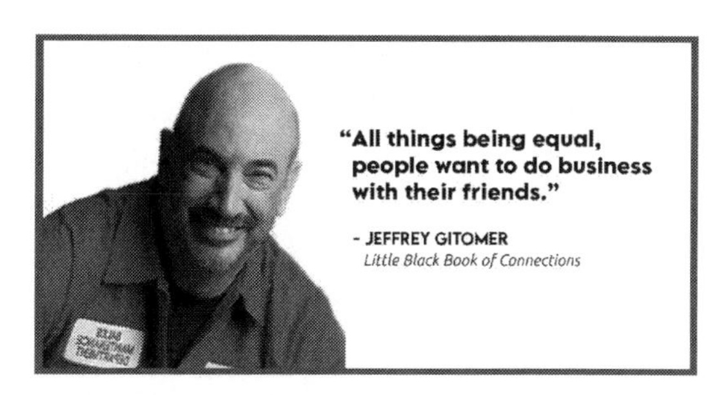

Raving Referral Law #4:

Stellar Service Creates Stellar Success

The fourth law of generating *Raving Referrals* is that stellar service creates stellar success.

It should go without saying that the better you treat your clients, customers, and even your staff and assistants, the more success you will experience—both in terms of your personal income as well as your personal satisfaction and fulfillment.

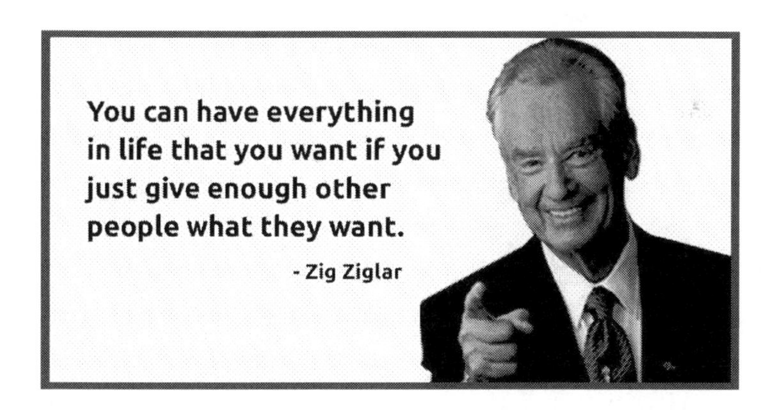

The more your clients and referral partners know how much you genuinely care about them and their success, the more they will care about you and your success.

The 5 Traits of Stellar Service:

When you serve clients exemplifying these five traits of stellar service, they will go out of their way to help you. In fact, they will rave about you each and every chance they get.

1. Listen intently to understand their cares and concerns
2. Communicate clearly
3. Meet and exceed expectations
4. Be on time and on budget
5. Always be in integrity

Be intentional about building a community of clients that are grateful for your service, generous with praise, and quick to recommend you to others. After all, word spreads quickly when you deliver stellar service to your clients. Soon, the only possible outcome is stellar success for you and your business.

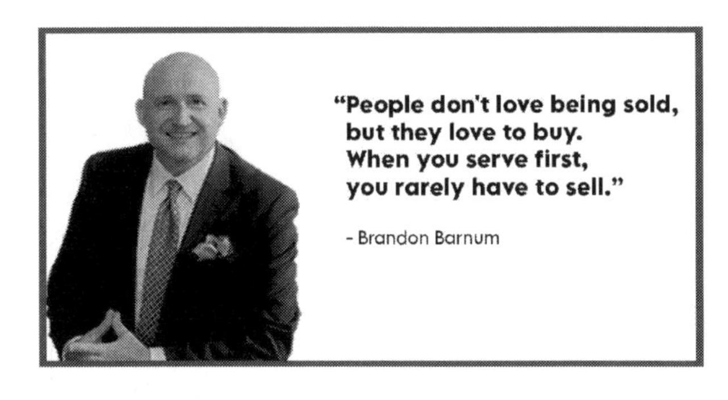

Raving Referral Law #5:

Delighted Clients Refer Delightful Clients

Wow your clients and referrals will follow.

The fifth law of *Raving Referrals* is that when you go above and beyond to delight your clients, they will happily and consistently refer you delightful clients.

Decades of empirical research shows that referred prospects:

- Trust you faster
- Refer more often
- Are more loyal
- Are more profitable
- Are more eager to meet with you
- Are often pre-sold on hiring you
- Are more enjoyable to work with

When you add all of these factors together, it's no wonder why delighted clients refer delightful clients!

As your clients praise you to others, they actually transfer the trust they've built with others onto you. Every time that happens, your new prospect's confidence in you and comfort with you grows.

Your goal should be for your clients to rave about you and your business with so much reverence and appreciation that the people they promote you to have already decided to do business with you... even before you've ever heard their name.

Of course, attracting *Raving Referrals* to delightful clients can only happen when you follow law number 6.

Raving Referral Law #6:

The Fortune is in the Follow-Up

When it comes to success for service businesses and professionals, your fortune will be made or lost based on how well you follow-up with people. In fact, follow-up is the single best way to double your referrals in a very short time.

Why? Because so few people actually do it. That means it's easy for you to stand out from your competition. Plus, it's a great demonstration of how well you follow-through and get the job done right.

If you really want a steady stream of *Raving Referrals*, you want to become famous for your follow-up.

Herbert True, a marketing specialist at Notre Dame University, found that:

- 44% of all salespeople quit following-up after the first call
- 24% quit following-up after the second call
- 14% quit following-up after the third call
- 12% quit following-up after the fourth call

That means 94% of all salespeople quit after the fourth call, yet 60% of all sales are made after the fourth call.

Plus, the more you update people as you serve them and the clients they refer, the more trust and confidence you build and the more referrals you will receive. Even if it's just a quick text, voice message, email, or social media message. Follow-up and watch the money start flowing to you faster.

If you really want to drive sales, follow-up with everyone who gives you a...

- Referral
- Introduction
- Testimonial
- Rating or Review

The more valuable the gift someone is giving you, the more important it is to follow-up with them. Be sure to thank them and give them updates so they have all the information they need and want.

As we mentioned earlier, when calculating your *Referral Score*, this practice is especially important when you receive a referral from a referral partner or professional colleague. When they trust you enough to serve their valuable clients, you have an incredible opportunity to deepen that relationship by following up with them. These updates demonstrate a high level of professionalism and continually build trust and collaboration.

Call your partners with regular updates on the status of each client they refer you. That way, they will always know exactly how you are helping their clients.

It also gives you an opportunity to ask, "Is there anyone else you'd like me to help?"

When you follow-up famously, you'll be amazed how many *Raving Referrals* you receive.

Raving Referral Law #7:

Everyone Wins, or No One Wins

The seventh and final law of generating *Raving Referrals* is that everyone wins, or no one wins.

When it comes to serving clients and building profitable partnerships with other professionals who serve your perfect prospects, it's important you ensure they always feel like they win every time they do business with you.

That requires that you strategically design your business practices, operations, and communications to guarantee that people know you have their best interests at heart.

Find ways to help them win.

Praise your clients, employees, and partners publicly whenever possible. People love recognition, so give them a shout out in your newsletter, website, email, or social media accounts.

Reward clients and referral partners who refer you. Even if it's simply with a discount, gift certificate, or free service with your business, they will feel honored, valued, and appreciated. This will boost the likelihood they will refer you again in the future.

Offer to cross-promote and recommend your partners to your clients, colleagues, and social sphere to help them attract more profitable prospects for their business.

The more people feel like they win every time they do business with you, the more business they will do with you... and the more *Raving Referrals* they will send your way.

To review, the 7 Laws of *Raving Referrals* are:

1. Every Referral Starts with Trust
2. The More You Give, The More You Receive
3. Relationships Trigger Transactions
4. Stellar Service Creates Stellar Success
5. Delighted Clients Refer Delightful Clients
6. The Fortune is in The Follow-Up
7. Everyone Wins, or No One Wins

As you master these seven laws and integrate them into your business, you will generate a steady stream of *Raving Referrals* for years to come.

For a quick summary of the 7 Laws of Raving Referrals, scan the QR code below or visit the link below:

ravingreferrals.com/7laws/

CHAPTER 3

Perfect Prospects & Lifetime Clients

Perfect Prospect Profile

Have you ever heard someone describe another person so vividly that you instantly thought of someone you know who's just like them? That's exactly what your goal is with your *Perfect Prospect Profile.*

To empower others with the ability to refer quality clients quickly and consistently, you must create a *Service Statement* that paints a clear picture of precisely who you help and how you help them.

As you practice and perfect describing your *Perfect Prospects* and your *Service Statement*, you can start sharing a clear, concise statement that will stick in the minds of people you meet. They will have no choice but to think of you the next time someone is describing the challenge that you solve.

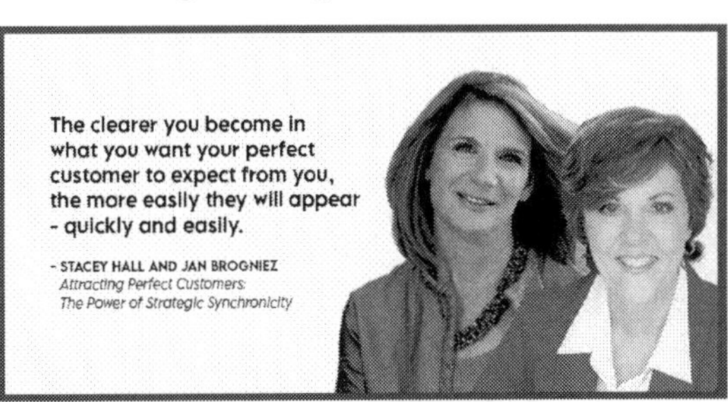

Quality Over Quantity

When it comes to referrals, it's better to have high-quality referrals to qualified candidates who actually need and want the service or solution you provide. After all, introductions to people who don't match your preferred profile can be a total waste of time and energy for both them and for you.

Your goal is to describe your *Perfect Prospects* to clients and referral partners, so they easily understand, remember, and scout for people who match your target. Your *Service Statement* gives them the ability to retell your story to others so their desire to do business with you increases before you've even spoken with them.

Once you've accomplished that, you will have enlisted them as *Referral Champions* scouting for you and singing your praises to the precise people you are looking to serve.

The Two Parts to Your Perfect Prospect Profile Are:

1. Who you help
2. How you help

Once you get clear on these two things, the final step is to write your *Service Statement* and start sharing who you help and how you help as a story. That way people can tell your *Service Statement* and story each time they are talking to one of your Perfect Prospects. So, let's go through each of these in detail, starting with who you help.

Who You Help

Take a moment to think about the best clients you've ever had throughout your entire career; the type of client where if you could attract more exactly like these, you'd be beyond thrilled, and so would they.

Can you picture them right now? If I were to ask you the names of your five best clients, who would they be? Take a moment to write down their names now.

My 5 Best Clients Have Been:

1. ________________________________
2. ________________________________
3. ________________________________
4. ________________________________
5. ________________________________

What Makes Them Your Best Clients?

- Why did these people come to mind?
- What do they have in common?
- Were they your most profitable clients, the most enjoyable, or somewhere in between?
- Is there a specific type of client who uses your services most frequently?
- What common goals, needs, or challenges do they share?
- What type of people give you the most referrals and introductions?
- How often do your ideal clients use your services?
- How much revenue do your ideal clients typically represent to you?

The answers to these questions should start to reveal some commonalities you can use to build your *Perfect Prospect Profile*. The clearer that you are, the easier it is for others to refer you effectively and consistently.

Homeowners and Consumers

If you typically serve consumers or homeowners as we do at HOA.com, how would you describe your ideal clients when factoring in their:

- Age
- Gender
- Income
- Location
- Stage of Life
- Marital Status
- Parental Status
- Homeownership Status
- Occupation, Hobbies, or Passions

Maybe your ideal client is a single mom in her 30s who loves yoga, cooking, and dancing. Or perhaps it is a grandparent over 60 who is getting ready to retire and relocate.

The more specific you are, the more clearly you can describe the type of people you are looking to serve. Your job is to make it easy for others to introduce and refer you to people who are a great fit for the services and solutions you provide. That will lead to more profitable prospects coming your way.

Businesses and Business Owners

If you serve businesses or business owners, you may want to target specific prospects who meet certain characteristics such as their:

- Title
- Industry

- Annual Revenue
- Years in Business
- # of Employees and/or Locations
- Type of Products or Services They Provide

Maybe you're looking to connect with a specific position within a company like the CEO, HR director, procurement officer, or sales manager. If so, be sure to let people know. They may have a friend, family member, or close contact who matches your *Perfect Prospect Profile.*

If you serve businesses or business owners, perhaps your Perfect Prospect is a CEO of a medium-sized manufacturing company with 50 or more employees and sales of over $10 million. Or maybe you are only looking to connect with branch managers of banks, credit unions, finance companies, or mortgage lenders.

Whatever the case may be, communicating a clear description of precisely who you are looking to serve will help your *Referral Champions* make high-quality introductions.

How You Help

Once you have clarity around what your ideal client looks like, next you need to define how you help them.

- What are the biggest problems you solve for your clients?
- What specific outcomes, goals, or objectives do you help your ideal clients achieve?
- What do you think is most important to your ideal clients?
- What are your best client success stories?

These questions will help you get clear on how best to describe the challenges you solve and the solutions you provide.

Write Your Service Statement

Once you've gotten crystal clear on who you help and how you help them, it's time to write your *Service Statement*.

This is a description of your business you will share over and over in one-on-one meetings, at networking events, and professional functions. Your *Service Statement* will help paint a clear picture in the mind of the person you are talking to so they immediately think of people who might need your services.

We recommend you follow our DREAM formula to ensure your *Service Statement* is:

- Descriptive
- Relatable
- Engaging
- Authentic
- Memorable

Example Service Statement

To help you better understand what a powerful service statement looks like, here is an example of a *Service Statement* for a business coach:

> *"You know how some businesses get stuck and struggle to grow past a certain point? I specialize in helping dental practices increase case acceptance, optimize employee engagement and increase profitability by an average of 30% in the first 12 months.*
>
> *So, if you know any dental practice who are looking to increase their revenues and profits, I'd love to help them. Does anyone come to mind right now?"*

In the example above, the business coach identified that she is looking to serve dental practices.

This gives the listener important data they can use to scan their memory banks and think about the dentists they know. Everyone has a dentist, so at the very least, the person will refer their own dentist.

Once the listener meets a dentist in the future, they will quickly recall the coach's scenario and recommend the business coach to the dentist.

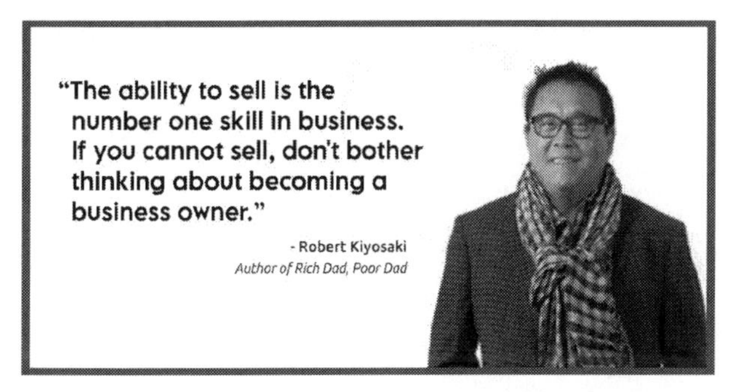

Get Started Now

Take a few moments to describe a challenge that your ideal clients face. Then describe your solution in a way that tells a story the person will understand and remember. That way, they will immediately think of you and refer them to you.

Just fill in the blanks to create your *Service Statement:*

You know how ________________________________

____

(Describe Your Ideal Clients and the Challenges they Face)

Well, I help ________________________________

____

solve/achieve ________________________________

____

Practice saying it out loud in the mirror once you've created a *Service Statement* you feel good about until it becomes completely comfortable and natural. Then, once you've mastered the mirror, ask a colleague or referral partner if you can share it with them. As you test it out on a few people, be sure to ask for their honest feedback.

Are there any refinements or improvements you want to make now that you've used it in a conversation and heard it out loud?

Was your statement clear as to who you help and how you help? Was it memorable? Ask them to restate what they heard so you can listen to how they describe your services.

Is there anyone they think of right now who matches your *Perfect Prospect Profile*? You might just attract some *Raving Referrals* just by practicing your *Service Statement*.

As you practice and perfect sharing who you help and how you help with others, the more comfortably and powerfully you'll be able to share it. Over time, more and more people will understand exactly who you help and how you help.

Lifetime Client Value

Each client you serve is worth far more than the value of that single transaction or service call. After all, when you service your clients exceptionally well, they will do business with you for years to come and refer you to others frequently.

I learned that first-hand back in the mortgage business. Although I would earn an average of $3,000 per loan funded, I realized each client was really worth over $10,000 on average throughout the lifetime of each client relationship.

Clients would come to me for multiple loans over time, whether it be to buy a new home, refinance their existing home, or invest in a vacation or rental property. Plus, they would refer me to their friends, family, co-workers, and clients who I was happy to help.

To calculate out your Lifetime Client Value, just multiple the average income you earn per transaction, times the number of transactions each client averages with you, times the number of good referrals each client gives you.

$ __________	Earnings Per Transaction
X __________	# of Lifetime Transactions
X __________	# of Referrals They Give
$	Lifetime Client Value

For example, if your average transaction represents $100 per service call, and you service each client once per month (or 12 transactions per year), that client is worth $1,200 to your business annually.

If your typical client uses your services an average of three years or 36 months, each client then represents $3,600 in revenue over the lifetime of their client engagement.

Referrals are the accelerator that really drives your revenue and business. If each client refers you just one additional client with a similar monthly service plan, your initial client has now delivered an additional $3,600 in projected revenue to your business.

Understanding the total value that each new client represents to your business over time can change your perspective and appreciation for them in a hurry. It also determines how many marketing dollars you can afford to spend to acquire each new customer.

After all, if you could spend $100 to gain a client worth $1,000 or even $10,000 to your business, how many times would you like to do that? As often as possible, right?

The key lesson here is to view each client not just by the one-time revenue you will earn from servicing them today. Through the perspective of the lifetime client value, you will earn by serving them and their referrals for years to come.

Danny Creed is a good friend of mine who also happens to be the six-time #1 global business coach for Bryan Tracy's Focal Point Coaching company. In Danny's book, *Thriving Business*, he states the fi ve most common marketing mistakes are:

1. No idea who the ideal customer is
2. No idea what the ideal customer wants
3. No idea as to what business you're really in
4. No idea why anyone should buy or what sets you apart from the competition
5. No idea how to explain your business in thirty seconds or less

If any of those is a gap for you, take a few minutes to get clear on each of these fi ve areas of your business.

Before long, you'll have *Raving Referrals* and introductions coming in consistently.

Creating your Perfect Prospect Profi le is an important step towards success. Scan the QR code or visit the link below to view a special video tip:

ravingreferrals.com/perfect_prospect

CHAPTER 4

Learn Why They Buy

For many people, closing or enrolling clients can be a challenge. So, what if there was a quick, easy, and effective way to increase your closing rate up to 300%?

There is when you learn people's **BANK**CODE and understand how each person thinks and how they make buying decisions.

The truth is that we human beings have twenty-four very different personality styles. Some people are naturally outgoing and friendly, greeting everyone they meet with a smile and a hug. These people excel in sales, customer service, and other positions where relationships matter.

Others are more shy and introverted, preferring to have as little human contact as possible. You probably know a number of these people, and perhaps that is how you were created. These people tend to be computer programmers, accountants, mechanics, electricians, plumbers, and other professions where they can excel working with things more than with people.

Take It to The B.A.N.K.

When it comes to the buying process, the same is true. When working with prospects and selling your products or services, some will use their intuition to assess your offer quickly. Others need time to analyze information on their various options to select the optimal solution before moving forward.

It's important to recognize people think differently based on their personality style. So, if people process information and make decisions much differently, why do most businesspeople use the exact same presentations and conversations for each prospect they meet?

This was a question I had never considered until October 14, 2017 when I was leading a 2-day event called the Profit Partner Summit where teaching this *Raving Referral* system to an audience of over 200 in Phoenix, Arizona. After walking off stage, a woman named Sandy approached me, introduced herself, handed me four colored cards, and said,

> *"Do me a favor: read the information on these cards and sort them in the order of what's most important to least important to you. That will help me serve you better and save us both time."*

After reviewing the cards, I quickly sorted and handed them back. What happened next blew me away.

As Sandy reviewed the order of the cards I handed her, she started describing my personality. I was shocked at how accurate her assessment was, and all I had done was sort four cards. I've taken at least a dozen different personality assessments, including Myers Briggs (MBTI), DiSC, The Harrison Assessment, and StrengthsFinder, to name a few. Each time, I had to go online and tediously answer 60-100 questions which typically took between 10-20 minutes. With **B.A.N.K.**, it was nearly instant, and there was no technology needed.

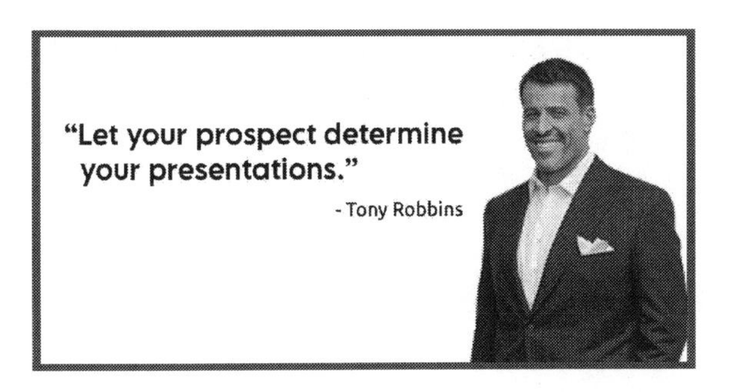

Sandy went on to explain how this **B.A.N.K.** system helps you close more sales in less time, increasing closing rates to as much as 300%. She also shared a white paper scientifically validating **B.A.N.K.** as the world's only sales methodology that accurately predicts buying behavior in real-time.

Close More Sales in Less Time

The key to increasing your sales conversion rates is to identify your prospect's personality type. Once you understand their **BANK**-CODE you can customize your conversations and presentations to be most effective based on how each person processes information and makes buying decisions. In just seconds, this easy and reliable system can help you:

- Supercharge Your Sales
- Transform Your Communications
- Make Lifelong Connections

Science long ago determined that four distinct primary personality types explain how we think, make decisions, and interact with the world. **B.A.N.K.** uses this personality science to help you improve interpersonal communication for better personal and professional relationships.

In 1992, the Chally Group conducted a research project known as the World Class Sales Project. They concluded that only 18% of buyers would buy from a salesperson who doesn't match the buyer's personality type. That's much lower than the 82% success rate when personality types are aligned.

The four **BANK**CODES are: Blueprint, Action, Nurturing, and Knowledge.

As you look at the following list, which would you choose as your top choice if you could only choose one?

BLUEPRINT	ACTION	NURTURING	KNOWLEDGE
Stability Structure Systems Planning Processes Predictability Responsibility Duty Rules Credentials Titles Tradition	Freedom Flexibility Spontaneity Action Opportunity Excitement Attention Stimulation Competition Winning Fun Image	Relationships Authenticity Personal Growth Significance Teamwork Involvement Community Charity Ethics Harmony Morality Contribution	Learning Intelligence Logic Self-Mastery Technology Research & Development Science Universal Truths Expertise Competence Accuracy The Big Picture

Now that you've identified your first choice, what would you choose next? Complete that process until you have your four-code combination and write that in the lines below:

____

____

____

____

Unlike other personality systems that are based on psychology, **B.A.N.K.** is the only values-based assessment that measures a person's "buyology." My fascination grew after Sandy emailed my 24-page **BANK**PASS report, which explained my personality in great detail. It outlined the triggers which get me to yes and the tripwires that lead me to say no in a sales setting. Beyond that, it helped me understand how to better connect and communicate with the other codes I had struggled with before.

Did you know there are 24 individual **BANK**CODES that drive why people buy? To learn the secrets, science and system to increase sales conversions up to 300%, visit:

https://ravingreferrals.com/bankcode/
or Scan the Code Below:

Instant Empathy

The market researcher in me needed to test the system and see what results it delivered. As I started using the cards at networking events and one-on-one meetings, I found people were as fascinated as I was. Each person I handed the cards to was happy to participate because the exercise was all about them. They were excited to share why they chose each card. It was amazing to watch these colorful cards quickly identify each person's personality in under 90 seconds.

What I soon realized was that **B.A.N.K.** gave me instant empathy. Within seconds of meeting someone, I cracked their code and immediately understood how their mind works. Best of all, it's fast, fun, and fascinating. People love talking about themselves, which creates the space where people open up, helping you understand them rapidly.

The most important code I ever cracked was for my daughter Ella. While we are incredibly close and have great daddy-daughter dates, our conversations have felt more like debates since she entered her teen years.

After cracking her **BANK**CODE and watching her select the Knowledge card first, everything suddenly clicked. Our codes are complete opposites, which helped me understand the space between us. Instantly I saw how my way of expressing myself completely repelled her because it didn't match the way her brain processes information. When we talk, her scientific mind goes to work analyzing for accuracy and application. If I make grandiose or generalized statements, her natural response is to question or challenge, which leaves me feeling criticized.

Because of **B.A.N.K.**, I now understand my daughter much better. Rather than trying to change her, I embrace and celebrate her strengths. Seeing her choose the Nurturing card last helped me understand why she rarely shows affection like she did when she was young. Now that I understand how her brilliant brain works, I truly appreciate the woman she was created to be.

It's been two years since cracking Ella's code, and our relationship has never been better. I'll be forever grateful for the understanding and empathy **B.A.N.K.** has given me.

To unlock the secrets, the science, and the system to supercharge your sales in less than 90 seconds, visit KnowYour-Code.US. You can also get great training on this powerful sales methodology at TheChampionsInstitute.com.

Referred to a Rockstar

Since this book is about generating *Raving Referrals*, I have to share that I was thrilled when Sandy called offering to introduce me to Cheri Tree, the creator of the program and author of the book, *Why They Buy*.

Over a series of phone calls, Cheri and I became fast friends and mutual admirers. Before long, we were collaborating and creating a strategic alliance to empower more people with **B.A.N.K.** We scheduled an interview and promoted her to my tribe. Then, as our respect and relationship grew, Cheri invited me to teach the *Raving Referrals* system to her audience at the international **B.A.N.K.** conference in Vegas. The following month, I invited her to join me at an Oscars after party at Universal Studios in L.A. with Ashton Kutcher and Matthew McConaughey as guests of honor.

Over the years that have followed, my respect and admiration for Cheri have grown immensely, and I believe the feeling is mutual. In my opinion, **B.A.N.K.** can help everyone improve their relationships and live better lives. That's why I am committed to supporting Cheri's mission to crack the code of every person on the planet.

To that end, I dedicated ten months of my life to helping her build and launch Codebreaker Technologies, including Codebreaker AI. This revolutionary technology enables you to crack personality codes in just one click using a LinkedIn profi le. It's an amazing tool that I recommend to anyone looking to close more sales and build better relationships.

Cheri agreed to let my readers try Codebreaker AI on a special $1 trial. To take advantage, visit OneDollarAITrial.com and use the promo code BANK. You can also scan the QR code below for instant access.

One of the reasons I share this example is that being referred to as influencers is a strategy you want to master. This will help you gain access to people you may otherwise never meet. In today's hyper-social world, just one referral can change your life.

The key is to follow up and follow through. Add value and help achieve whatever mission, dream, or goal they are passionate about. Then when you earn an influencer's trust and have given them tremendous value, they will feel indebted and naturally offer to promote. When they do, their celebrity endorsement elevates your expert status, which in turn boosts your referrals and revenues.

The question is, are you ready to boost your expert status? If so, you'll love what's coming next.

CHAPTER 5

Establish Your Expert Status

Establishing yourself as an expert is one of the most influential and strategic ways to build your business. It increases your credibility and visibility, which helps attract new clients and referral partners. Plus, if you don't share your expertise online, your competitors will be happy to step in and win over your clients.

When you look up the word "expert" in the Oxford dictionary, you'll find the definition reads, "a person who has a comprehensive and authoritative knowledge of or skill in a particular area."

While you may not feel like an expert, the truth is you have specialized knowledge that can help people improve their lives. You have mastered systems, strategies, tips, and tricks that can help them save time, save money, make money, improve their health, reduce stress, improve relationships, be a better parent, get a better job, or whatever it is you do to help people live better lives. When you realize that the purpose of your business is to make a difference to others, you can stand strong in your power, confidently sharing your wisdom with others.

One of the many inspiring authors I've had the pleasure of knowing is Debbie Allen, author of the book, *The Highly Paid Expert*. Debbie truly is an expert on becoming an expert. In her 2019 book, *Success Is Easy*, Debbie shares,

> *"What's great about being an expert is that while you are fulfilling your life's mission, you are also influencing and teaching others. As the expert, you can go deeper with your knowledge than the average person in your industry and develop a step-by-step blueprint, program, or system that can be duplicated by other people."*

To establish your expertise, consider posting and promoting the following on your website and social media channels, as well as displaying them throughout your office:

- Affiliations with Chambers of Commerce or the Better Business Bureau
- Articles or blogs you have written
- Associations to which you belong
- Awards you have received
- Boards on which you serve
- Books you have written or have been featured in
- Charities for which you volunteer or committees on which you serve
- Endorsements from vendors or suppliers
- Media interviews or coverage you have received
- Partners who have chosen to do business with you
- Photos with celebrities, authors, and influencers
- Testimonials from clients and customers

In addition to posting and displaying these examples of your expertise, you can also go live on social media, sharing quick tips for your Perfect Prospects. While it may seem intimidating at first, here's a simple formula you can follow to share your expertise:

- Introduce yourself, stating your name and company

- Describe the challenges you solve
- Emphasize the pain of not taking action
- Outline top options and solutions
- Share success stories
- Suggest next steps

Here's an example script to give you some ideas,

"Hello, this is Amy Andrews with Andrews Realty, here to give you my top five tips for new homeowners. I love helping clients buy their first home because there's nothing more satisfying than helping a family achieve the American dream of homeownership.

The challenge many people face is that as first-time homeowners, they often find themselves overwhelmed with all the new choices and responsibilities that come with owning a home for the first time. That's why I wanted to share my top five tips for first-time homeowners to help make your life a little easier as you move into your first home.

1. *Change the locks (share a sentence or two as to why they should follow each tip).*
2. *Do a deep clean.*
3. *Perform a home energy audit.*
4. *Replace air filters regularly.*
5. *Paint and make upgrades before you move in.*

These tips are great reminders even if you have owned your home for years. Recently, I helped a client named Sarah buy her first home, and she was so grateful for these tips because she scheduled a home energy audit, which reduced her energy bill by $500 per year. She even qualified for an energy efficiency tax credit.

If you ever need introductions to any home service professionals, I have a vetted, trusted network of professionals I am happy to recommend. That offer goes for your neighbors, friends, and family too. I'm always here to help and am never too busy to take care of the people you care about. Just have them call or text me at (123) 456-7890.

Thanks for watching, and remember, at Andrews Realty, we're committed to helping you reach your real estate goals. Whether you are looking to buy, sell, or invest, we're here to support your success."

If you're not sure where to start, simply search online for articles related to your industry. You will find countless books, blogs, strategies, and tips you already know and can easily teach your clients.

Now it's time to share that wisdom with the world. As you post your golden nuggets, you'll find that your clients and the social sphere will engage, ask questions, and request more information about your services. As if by magic, new client opportunities will appear as if they are drawn to you like a magnet. People you've never met will also share what you do with others, especially as you tell stories of the impact you make.

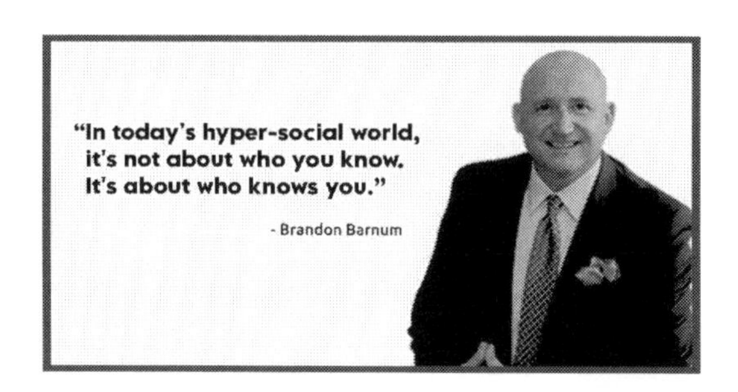

You can establish your expert status by creating a blog, podcast, video, special report, workshop, webinar, or book. The key is to constantly share your knowledge and wisdom online so you stay top of mind and elevate your status with everyone you can.

One of the most significant benefits of sharing your expertise on social media is that other influencers and business owners will ask to interview you to help their clients and social sphere. As they do, you may find some of them make excellent guests sharing their expertise with your audience. This is one of the most powerful strategies you can use to grow your referrals, which is why we will cover it in detail in Chapter 17 of this book as we outline the top *21 Top Cross Promotion Campaigns.*

Be Easy to Refer

To maximize the quality and quantity of *Raving Referrals* coming your way, it's critical you make yourself easy to refer.

Giving your clients, customers, referral partners, and social sphere an easy way to recommend, refer, and promote you is one of the fastest ways to grow your business.

When you think about your business, why would someone tell another person about you?

The answer is likely different than you imagine. The fact of the matter is most people don't care about you or your business the way you do. Their motivation for recommending you is primarily to solve the problems and challenges for the people they care about. Your job is to make it quick and easy for them to spread the word about your business far and wide so you can attract as many profitable prospects as possible.

When people have a referral for you, what are you asking them to do?

If you're sitting there stymied by that question, that means you have a big gap in your business. You are making them do all the work and creating barriers between you and your ideal clients. The simple truth is that business development is your job. It's not your client's or customer's job. So why do you make them work to give you business?

Just check out this rack card we give out for HOA.com. This is a great leave behind that gives people our website, toll-free phone number and even a QR code they can scan with their mobile phone.

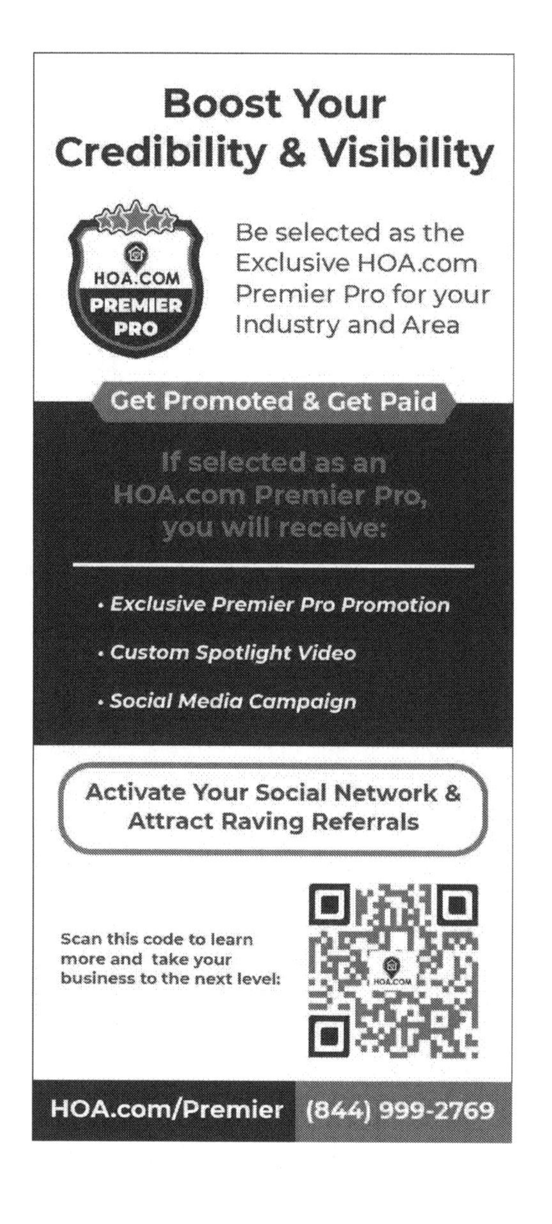

One of the biggest gaps I see when coaching clients to get more referrals is that they have no system in place for their referrals. I've surveyed thousands of business owners and found that less than 10% actually have a system in place to ask, receive, track, and follow up on the referrals they receive. That means nine out of ten of you have a serious gap that is costing you money each and every day. That's why you need to develop a *Referral Kit* for your business.

Your Referral Kit

Your *Referral Kit* is something tangible you give your clients and referrals partners to share when recommending you. Simply package your expertise as a special report, book, video, or brochure that explains the challenge you solve, the possible solutions clients should consider, and a specific call-to-action, so they contact you for assistance. This elevates your authority in the mind of your prospect, which instantly boosts trust.

Using this strategy, you can dramatically increase your revenue per client too. That's because your *Referral Kit* will increase the number of prospects you attract while simultaneously boosting your average revenue per client once they view you as a trusted expert.

The good news about creating your *Referral Kit* is that you only have to do it once, and you can use it for the rest of your career. The easiest way to create your *Referral Kit* is to compile blogs you've written into a book or special report. If you haven't written any blogs, you can use the Frequently Asked Questions section of your website to get started.

Another great option is to record an interview and have the audio recording transcribed. Simply coordinate a conversation with one of your business or referral partners via zoom or Facebook Live.

Then download the video file and upload it to one of the many online transcription services like Temi.com or Otter.ai.

Once you package and publish your expertise through your *Referral Kit*, you boost your influencer status, which will lead people to seek you out. After all, your *Referral Kit* elevates your status from being seen as a salesperson to an industry expert.

That was my experience after Mark Victor Hansen and Robert Allen featured me in their best-selling book, *Cracking the Millionaire Code,* back in 2005. Once that book was published, I had prospective clients calling and contacting me from around the world. They were eager to do business with me because these global authorities and influencers had established my expertise before I had ever spoken with these people. Sixteen years later, people still reach out to me after reading that book.

Give the Gift of You

The goal of your *Referral Kit* is to give your referral champions a turn-key tool they can use to promote your services easily, effortlessly, and effectively. When they share your *Referral Kit*, you educate your audience, elevate your status, and reduce sales pressure. These factors all attract profitable prospects who will schedule with you quickly and consistently.

You can even present your *Referral Kit* as a gift. Once you package your expertise in a special report or book, your referral partners can give it as a gift for each of their clients and customers. They are looking to help and add value to their clients, so if you give them a way to do that by introducing your expertise, it creates a win–win–win scenario where everyone benefits.

That's exactly what I did with *Cracking the Millionaire Code*. That book became my personal brochure. Every time I met a new prospect, I gave them a copy of the book along with my business card inserted on page 42, where my three-page bio began. Even if they never read a word of the book, the simple fact that these literary giants had endorsed and written about me established my expertise and trustworthiness. Plus, it became an easy way for people to recommend me to their clients and contacts.

Creating your own *Referral Kit* and establishing your expertise will elevate your status and accelerate trust. The key is to make it easy for others to refer you in a way that makes you the most trusted option in the eyes of your partners and prospects. Once you do that, you are on your way to attracting *Raving Referrals* for years to come.

Truth be told, that was one of my primary drivers for writing this book. Although I've been teaching these strategies for over a decade, I needed a better way to pass on my knowledge and give people a better way of sharing my message with the world. Not only that, writing this book gave me an opportunity to connect and collaborate with over 100 experts and influencers we are featuring in this book, training courses, and social promotion campaigns.

That truly is the beauty of this *Raving Referrals* program. As you put this system and these strategies to work in your business, you will build a growing group of referral partners and loyal clients who will gladly refer profitable prospects to you quickly and consistently.

The Appreciation Challenge

Giving is the key that unlocks receiving. The more you give, the more you will receive.

Be on the lookout for ways to give to people you care about and those you're looking to build profitable partnerships with or attract referrals from. The more time and energy you invest in your key connections and meaningful relationships, the more relational equity you build, which will generate opportunities for years to come.

One of the fastest, easiest, and most powerful things you can do to add value is to simply appreciate them. That's why we challenge you to show some appreciation right now.

The Rules:

1. Look through the contacts on your mobile phone.
2. Choose the top 10 people you want to build relational equity with.
3. Text or send a direct message or personalized video expressing your genuine appreciation for them.
4. Complete this exercise within 1 hour of reading these instructions.
5. Don't ask anything of them in return. Just give them some love.
6. Don't even ask them to respond to you. It's as easy as that!

Appreciation Examples:

- Been thinking about you and wanted you to know how much I appreciate you.
- Thanks for all you are and all you do. I appreciate you!
- Someone asked me to think of people I appreciate, and you immediately came to mind. Just wanted to let you know I appreciate you. Have a great day.
- Thank you for always_______________. I appreciate you.
- Have I told you lately you inspire me?
- I just wanted you to know I was reading some of your social posts and really appreciate how you show up in the world.
- I thought you would like to know I was just thinking about the people I admire most, and you are at the top of my list. Thanks for being you.

- I just wanted you to know how much I respect and admire you. You inspire me.

As you text your expressions of appreciation, you'll be amazed at the response you will receive. People will be blown away because they don't hear unsolicited praise very often. As you show your appreciation for them, they will naturally thank you for your kind words. Often, this will lead to opportunities to connect and discuss the possibility of a profitable partnership.

So have fun and spread the love right now!

Seriously. Stop reading and **DO THIS RIGHT NOW.** It's one of the easiest ways to quickly start a conversation with someone you admire who can make a diff erence to you personally and professionally. It only takes a few minutes, so put a bookmark in this page and spread the love. You'll be glad you did, and so will those you reach out to.

Now that we've covered the *Raving Referral* basics, it's time to give you the secrets and the science to engaging and activating your referral network, so they become your referral champions.

Scan the QR code or visit the link below for quick tips on establishing your expert status:

https://ravingreferrals.com/expertise

CHAPTER 6

Engage Your Referral Champions

As a business owner or professional, the level of your success is mainly dependent on your ability to attract *Raving Referrals*. The more recommendations you receive from clients and your social sphere, the faster your business will grow and the more prosperity you will achieve. That's why it's so important to engage your network systematically in a way that transforms them into *Referral Champions* for you and your business. Then, the more you celebrate, thank, and reward your *Referral Champions*, the more *Raving Referrals* you will receive.

Most business owners struggle their entire career trying to attract prospects by marketing to strangers. They spend tens of thousands of dollars on ineffective marketing, wasting hundreds of hours talking to people who will never deliver any real value to their business.

The truth is that you're sitting on an untapped goldmine of profitable prospects you can access quickly and consistently. This section will share a time-tested way to have your network deliver profitable prospects to you on a silver platter.

Even if you struggle with networking and are uncomfortable promoting yourself, the system, strategies, and scripts outlined here will give you a simple and scalable way to create predictable profitability for your practice or business.

Who do you know,
Who knows people,
You want and need to know?

The 3 Sources of Raving Referrals

The vast majority of referrals come from one of the following three groups of people:

1. Your Clients
2. Your Social Sphere
3. Complimentary Businesses and Professionals

Each of these groups can be an incredible source of referrals. While each group needs a slightly different approach to activate them into *Referral Champions* for your business, the overall strategy is very similar.

Your Clients

Current and past clients can be your #1 best source of referrals. That's because they have personally experienced and benefited from your product or service. When they share their story, and testimonial about the difference you made for them, the people the recommend to you automatically trust you more, which increases the likelihood they will use your service.

The key here is to consistently communicate to your clients through phone calls, text messages, email, direct mail, social media messages, and client appreciation events, so they feel the love over and over. Then, when you hear someone is looking for the service you provide, they will naturally and passionately recommend you and your company.

Your Social Sphere

Your social sphere includes all the people you interact with in your life, including your friends, family members, co-workers, and contacts. The truth is you should be promoting your services to everyone who is in your contact relationship management (CRM), email programs, phone contacts, and social media connections. Imagine how many more referrals you would attract to your business if you just stayed in touch with all the people you have met and hired for various services in your life. You are literally three feet from gold, and it's time you started mining it.

As you look over the list on the following pages, start thinking about people you know in each of these industries and categories:

Accountants
Account Managers
Advertising Managers
Appraisers
Appliance Repair People
Architects
Athletes
Attorneys
Authors
Auto Mechanics
Babysitters
Bakers
Bankruptcy Attorneys
Bartenders
Bookkeepers
Business Brokers
Business Coaches
Business Development Managers
Business Managers
Business Owners
Career Coaches
Carpet Cleaners
Car Salespeople
CEOs
Charities
Chefs
Church Members
College Alumni
Concierges
Consultants
Contractors
Copywriters
Counselors
Credit Repair Experts
Cyber Security Experts
Daycare Providers
Dentists
Divorce Attorneys
Dog Groomers
Drycleaners
Drywallers
Engineers
Entrepreneurs
Escrow Officers
Estate Planning Attorneys
Event Managers
Executives
Family Members
Financial Planners
Firefighters
First Responders
Flooring Installers
Florists
Franchise Consultants
Friends
Fundraisers
Furniture Salespeople
Golf Pros
Graphic Designers
Hair Stylists
Handymen
Healthcare Professionals
Health Coaches
High School Friends
Home Builders
Home Healthcare Providers
Home Inspectors
Hotel Managers
House Cleaners
Human Resource Managers
Influencers
Insurance Agents
Interior Designers
Investors

Jewelers
Goverment Employees
Grocers
Landscapers
Leasing Agents
Life Coaches
Manicurists
Marketing Consultants
Mediators
Mortgage Loan Officers
Movers
Musicians
Nurses
Nutritionists
Optometrists
Office Managers
Painters
Paramedics
Pastors
Pediatricians
Personal Trainers
Pest Control Technicians
Pharmacists
Photographers
Plumbers
Police Officers
Politicians
Pool Cleaners
PR Agents
Printers
Programmers
Project Managers
Property Managers
Public Speakers
Real Estate Agents
Relationship Managers
Rental Agents
Reporters
Restaurant Owners
Roofers
Salespeople
Sales Trainers
Secretaries
Security Guards
Software Designers
Swimming Instructors
Seminar Attendees
Skin Care Specialists
Social Media Consultants
Surgeons
Tax Advisors
Teachers
Technology Experts
Tennis Pros
Travel Agents
Waiters and Watresses
Web Designers
Writers
Veterans
Veterinarians
Virtual Assistants
Yoga Instructors
Youth Sports Coaches

As you look over this list, you're undoubtedly thinking of people you know who should know about your business. If you have their contact information, start communicating with them regularly about the products and services you provide. After all, you never know when they or someone they know will need what you offer. If you aren't marketing to them consistently and staying top-of-mind, someone else will be glad to serve them and win their business.

You may be looking at this list thinking, "I would never want to approach these people about my business." If so, that may be part of the reason you don't yet have the results you desire and deserve. Don't let your ego get in the way of your success. This is not the time to be shy. Your family's future success is at stake. Be confident and bold, knowing you provide great value to everyone you serve.

I learned long ago that you could either be right, or you can be rich. It's your choice, so choose wisely. If you are committed to success, spread the word far and wide about the services you provide. After all, nothing ventured, nothing gained.

You have absolutely nothing to lose. If you email or contact people and they aren't interested in doing business with you, they will simply ignore your message and move on. That said, by keeping your name and brand top of mind, they are much more likely to use your services and recommend you in the future.

Complementary Businesses and Professionals

While your past clients and social sphere are incredibly important, in my experience, you can build your business exponentially faster and larger by partnering with complementary business owners and professionals who serve your ideal clients. This strategy is so powerful that over half of this book is dedicated to teaching you how to achieve wealth and prosperity by partnering and cross-promoting with people who are serving your perfect prospects each and every day.

As you look back at the *Social Sphere* list we just covered, you probably see at least ten industries or professions that make their living serving the exact clients you are looking to attract. All you need is one solid partnership in each of those industries to create predictable profitability for your business.

I've personally closed over $500 million in business using this strategy, so I am here to tell you emphatically that it works when you work it. As a single dad back in my twenties, I was earning over $50,000 per year from just one referral partner alone. Imagine what you can achieve for your business when you follow the *Raving Referrals* system and *Referral Partner Blueprint* to create ten or more referral partnerships over the next year or two.

By collaborating and co-marketing with these people, you will help them grow their business while they help you grow yours.

Best of all, as you prove yourself to them and their clients, you will become an invaluable ally they can't live without. You will earn more and more of their business over time until, eventually, you will become the number one go-to expert to which they refer all of their clients and colleagues.

Your Network Drives Your Net Worth

We will teach you everything you need to know about creating profitable partnerships in Chapter 12 of this book. Then, in Chapter 17, we will outline the Top 21 Cross-Promoting Campaigns you can deploy with your referral partners. First, let's cover how to build your database and stay top of mind with each of the three sources or *Raving Referrals.*

Compile Your Database

If you're serious about success, building a database of your past clients, complementary professionals, and social sphere is paramount. All of your contacts should be centralized in one contact relationship management (CRM) system to make it easy for you to consistently communicate with your network.

That means importing your contacts from your phone as well as your Apple Mail, Gmail, Outlook, Yahoo Mail, and LinkedIn connections into one centralized communications command center. You also want to ensure you have all of your current and past clients as well as any and all prospects in your CRM.

If you don't yet have a CRM, check out RavingReferralsCRM.com for a powerful low-cost solution that is easy to activate and comes customized with funnels and campaigns for several top industries that serve homeowners and business owners.

Create Lifetime Clients

If you are serious about winning clients for life, it's imperative you keep your brand top-of-mind. Your goal is to become the top-trusted solution in your industry, so people always use your services and tell everyone they know to do the same.

Once your contacts are centralized, be sure to schedule a regular message to your market every month at a minimum. Consistently keep your brand and services in front of your database through regular printed or emailed newsletters as well as through your social media channels.

Here are some great segments and ideas for what to feature in your newsletters and social posts:

- Articles and Blogs
- Awards and Recognition
- Charity Collaborations
- Client Appreciation Events
- Client Success Stories
- Community Impact Campaigns
- Company Announcements
- Holiday Highlights
- Industry Updates
- Inspirational Quotes
- Membership Opportunities
- New Employee Introductions
- Product and Service Announcements and Training
- Referral Partner Spotlights
- Raving Rewards
- Referral Shout-Outs
- Special Offers
- Technology Innovations
- Testimonials
- Tips and Tricks
- Training Events
- Trends and Statistics

We will go into detail on how to communicate and cross-promote to your network in a later chapter. For now, the key is to get all of your contacts into one centralized CRM and schedule a regular message or newsletter to your database at least once per month.

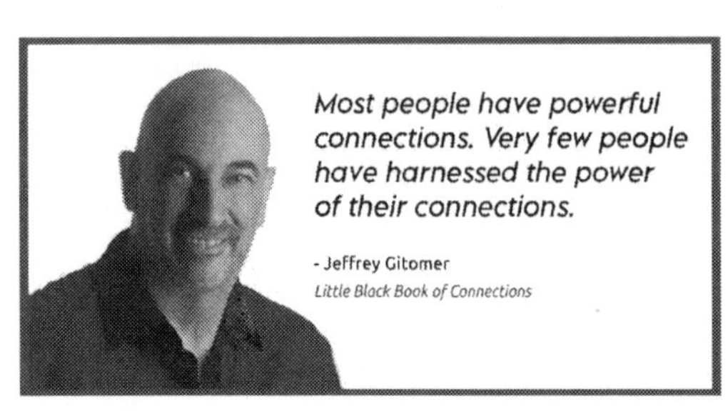

Survey For Success

One of the fastest and easiest ways to uncover opportunities for your business is by sending out a *Referability Survey* to your clients, colleagues, and social sphere. Surveying your clients and professional network will help you:

1. Spread the word about your business
2. Gain valuable feedback and insights into how people view you
3. Capture testimonials you can use in your marketing
4. Uncover opportunities to create profitable partnerships
5. Generate referrals right on the spot

Best of all, a *Referability Survey* will help you achieve all of this quickly. In fact, you can send out your survey in as little as ten minutes.

Creating Your Referability Survey

The fastest and easiest way to survey your social sphere is using the survey tools in Facebook, LinkedIn, or wherever you have a social following. There are also some great free software tools to help you quickly and easily send a survey. JotForm.com and

Qualtrics.com allow you to survey your clients and customers to capture ratings, reviews, and testimonials.

Creating a *Referability Survey* is as simple as asking people to rate you on a scale from 1-5 on how they view your:

- Trustworthiness
- Subject Matter Expertise
- Quality of Work
- Professionalism
- Responsiveness

Sending a survey is super easy and only takes a few minutes. Follow the simple instructions, import or sync your contacts, and then select the specific people you want your survey sent to. Once your list is ready to go, customize your questions and message, then press send.

Your message should include the fact that your business is in growth mode, so they know you are looking for additional clients. You can simply say something like:

> *"As one of my valued connections, I'd like to ask for your help. I'm working on growing my business and have a quick survey I'd like you to complete. It's totally anonymous and should only take about 30 seconds. This will give me some important feedback, so I'd really appreciate it if you would take a moment to do it now."*

Then, for best results, add a thank you message that says,

> *"Thanks for sharing your feedback. Before you go, if someone you know was asking about me or the services I provide, what would you tell them?"*

That last question is specifically designed to capture testimonials. Hopefully, you will get some great feedback and client success stories or quotes you can use on your website and in your marketing collateral. You may even find people recommend or refer you right then and there because someone they know needs your services now.

Once your message says what you want, just press send, then sit back and watch the results roll in. If you send your survey to a large list, you should start seeing some completed surveys within minutes.

Value Your VIPs

You likely have some VIP clients who use you often, refer you regularly, and account for a large percentage of your overall revenue in your business. After coaching and consulting thousands of entrepreneurs and professionals over the years, I can tell you that the 80/20 rule is very real. What I mean is that for many people, 80% of their business comes from 20% of their clients and referral partners. These people should be treated like gold because they can represent tens or hundreds of thousands of dollars to your bottom line.

After my second year in the mortgage business, I analyzed all of the loans I had closed and commissions I had earned to that point. I was surprised to find that just one of my realtors, named Dana Berry, had referred 25% of my total income for the year. That one relationship alone brought me over $50,000 in annual income which made her my #1 VIP from that point on.

Once I had identified just how lucrative that relationship was, I happily invested into co-marketing advertising campaigns with Dana in *The Real Estate Book* because I knew that every client she attracted would be referred my way. Even though I rarely got a single call from our joint ads, buyers who called Dana about one of her listings would consistently be referred to me to be prequalified before she would take them out to tour properties.

Best of all, Dana was an awesome woman who I loved spending time. We would regularly go out to lunch, happy hour, movies, and concerts. That's part of the beauty of building referral partnerships. You get to build your business with people who become some of your closest friends and allies.

Take a moment to think about your business. Over the past year, who has referred you the most business or the best clients? Do you have some past clients who refer you more than others? If so, make sure you show them some appreciation.

Thank and Update Your Referral Champions

When people refer you, be sure to communicate with your customers throughout the process so they are always up to date. It's better to over-communicate rather than leave them wondering what's going on.

I learned this lesson back in 2005 after receiving a mortgage refinance referral from John Jones, a VP at Intel. John was definitely a VIP client. I helped him finance and then later refinance his primary home, as well as a vacation home he acquired. In addition to the thousands of dollars in commissions I earned from serving him personally, he regularly referred other Intel employees and executives to me. That's where I made one of my all-time biggest business blunders.

A couple of months after referring one of his colleagues to me, John asked how things had gone with his associate. Excitedly I said something like, *"Just great. We closed on his loan two weeks ago, so he is a happy camper."* To which he replied, *"Let me give you a tip.*

When someone refers business to you, it's a really good idea to follow up with the person and let them know what happened."

My stomach dropped, and I felt like a total idiot. I couldn't believe I had been so dumb as to not update my VIP on the status of the client he had referred to me. If the referral had come from one of my referral partners, I absolutely would have kept them updated, but because it came from a client, the thought never even crossed my mind.

Needless to say, I apologized profusely and thanked him for the lesson. Then I quickly printed branded thank you cards with my company logo and a "thank you for your referral" message on the front with a pre-written message and blank line inside to fill in the name of the client they had referred. We quickly trained our thirty loan officers to send these out every time they received a referral from anyone. Our goal was to thank them for the referral, so they felt the love. We also made sure our team kept them updated throughout the entirety of the transaction.

In the years since, I've asked thousands of professionals if they've ever given a referral to someone and never heard back from the person to which they referred their clients. Unfortunately, nearly 100% of the people I've surveyed have had that same experience.

It doesn't take long to make a quick call or even just send an update by text or direct message. Alerting the people who refer you business will make them grateful for the update in just a few seconds. This will lead them to view you as a dependable professional worthy of sending their clients, colleagues, family, and friends to.

Send Video Messages & GIFs

When it comes to following up with people, one of the best ways to make a great impression is by recording and sending them a personalized video message. When you do, people will see your smiling face and be impressed that you are connecting in a way they likely haven't seen before. This personal touch takes only a few seconds and is much more impactful than sending a text, email, or direct message through a social platform. Simply record a quick video on your cell phone and text it to them like you would with a photo. If you are connected to them on Facebook or LinkedIn, you can record your video right on the messaging app and send over in seconds.

Another way to help your message stand out is to send them an animated or video GIF. These are entertaining, quick, and easy to send. Plus, they help you stand out and can make your contact smile or laugh feeling emotions they rarely experience through a simple text message. If you've never sent a video GIF, just find the GIF icon in your text messaging app and search for an image that conveys the message you want to send. For example, if you want to send someone a Happy Birthday message, search the term "Birthday." Then review and select the video GIF you think would best express the emotion you want to convey. Your message will make a lasting impression that will help you stand out from the crowd and build relationships faster.

Depending on the industry you are in, here are a few ways you can update your *Referral Champions*:

- Call and thank them once their referred party contacts you
- Send a thank you card naming the person they referred
- Text or email an update whether the person moves forward or not
- Share a photo of the work you performed
- Post the client's testimonial on social media, thanking and tagging your *Referral Champion*
- Send a thank you gift after the transaction has closed

- Call your *Referral Champion* after the transaction is closed, showing your appreciation, and asking if there is anyone else you can help

The amount of time, energy, and money you spend thanking your *Referral Champions* will vary based on your Lifetime Client Value. If a client only represents a few hundred dollars to you, a simple call or text will do. However, if the client means thousands of dollars to your business, you may want to go the extra mile to make sure your *Referral Champions* feel celebrated and rewarded.

The First Is the Worst

Do you remember the first time you tried to ride a bicycle? If you are like me, it felt scary, and you had visions of a disastrous painful crash. Most likely, you had a parent or family member assure you they would hold onto you, and everything would be fine. So, you pushed past the fear, grabbed the handlebars tight, and got up on that seat to face your fate.

As you anxiously started peddling, you pleaded with the person teaching you to not let go so you wouldn't fall and fail. They assured you everything would be fine, so you started your way down the street, sidewalk, or parking lot. After a few seconds, you started figuring out how to adjust your weight and balance the bike. One minute in, you had already learned the basics of riding a bike.

Then you had that joyous moment when you actually felt you were in control of the bike and would soon be racing down the street. For me, that was the moment I looked up to realize I was riding by myself, and no one was holding on to my bike any longer. That was the point when I over adjusted the handlebars and quickly crashed on the pavement. After realizing the pain of colliding with the concrete hurt far less than I imagined, I got up, dusted off my scrapped knees, and got back up determined to win. Needless to say, every other time I got on a bike after that experience, I was more confi dent than the fi rst time because I had learned what to do and what not to do.

The lesson here is that typically the fi rst time you do anything will be the absolute worst you will ever be at performing that task. After doing something new for the fi rst time, you get wiser and better because you will know what you did not know the fi rst time. It will feel easier. and you will be more comfortable because you will have learned some tips and tricks to improve your performance the second time around.

When it comes to engaging your *Referral Champions*, you just need to TAKE ACTION and get started. Fail forward as John Maxwell would say. The faster you TAKE ACTION, the faster you will find success. Just give yourself grace knowing the first is the worst and that every time after will get better and better.

Engaging your social sphere is one of the best ways to attract more *Raving Referrals*.

The good news is we are going to teach you how to create a *Raving Rewards* program in the next chapter.

Scan this QR code or visit the link below for a few quick tips on maximizing engagement through video:

https://ravingreferrals.com/engage/

CHAPTER 7

Create a Raving Rewards Program

R*eferral Rewards* can help you create a culture of referrals and automatically ask your clients, customers, and social sphere to actively refer you.

If you're like most professionals, you're probably really good at referring other people, but feel a little uncomfortable asking for referrals yourself. By adding a well-designed *Referral Rewards* campaign to your business or practice, you can systematize the process of asking for referrals and create a culture where asking for referrals is strategically added into all your client communications.

That's why *Referral Rewards* campaigns can be one of the fastest and easiest ways to attract more referrals from your clients and social sphere.

Just think about the success that companies like Dropbox and Uber have had building their brand as well as their business valuation simply by offering rewards to satisfied clients. Your goal is to incentivize others to share and promote your service with their friends, family, coworkers, and colleagues.

The truth is that as human beings, we are biologically wired to help other people. In fact, there's nothing more fulfilling than helping someone else. That's why people's sense of service is such a powerful motivator.

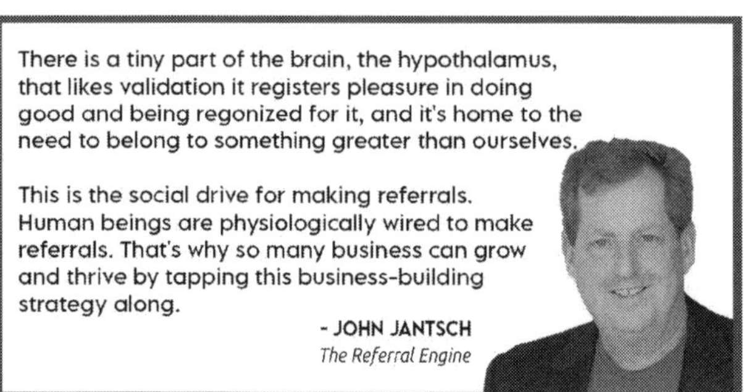

While your clients want to help you, their real motivation is wanting to help the people they care about improve their lives. If they feel like you can help people they know, they will be happy to refer them to you.

Adding a *Referral Rewards* program to your business helps you combine the satisfaction people get by helping you and their friends with an attractive reward or incentive for introducing their loved ones to you. This creates a powerful referral engine that can generate clients for years to come.

Designing Your Referral Rewards Program

When creating your *Referral Rewards* program, there are four things you will need to do, which include:

1. Choose a Program Type
2. Choose a Reward Type
3. Promote Your Program
4. Recognize and Reward Referrers

Let's walk through each of these steps so you can design the optimal program for your business.

1. Choose a Program Type

There are two main types of *Referral Rewards* programs you can choose from: *Referral Contests* and *Refer-A-Friend* programs.

Referral Contests – In referral contests, customers receive entries for each person they refer. This means the more referrals they give, the higher their probability to win. This strategy can produce the fastest results and highest return on investment as it creates a campaign with a deadline that can lead to immediate new client opportunities. That said, you will need to make the prize attractive enough to get people to refer others, as they won't automatically receive a benefit for recommending your business.

Refer-A-Friend Program – In these campaigns, you simply reward clients each time they refer someone to your business. This is basically like an affiliate program where you compensate people for promoting and referring you new business.

When designing your campaign, you need to consider:

- Do you want to reward clients for each referral they give you, or only when referrals turn into new clients or customers?
- Do you want to hold a short-term campaign, or create an ongoing referral campaign where customers always receive rewards when they refer you?

Both campaign types can be highly effective at driving referral activity. You simply need to decide what type of campaign will work best for your business. Either way, we will teach you how to promote and build buzz around your campaign.

2. Choose A Reward Type

The good news about running a *Referral Rewards* campaign is that your clients have a natural desire to refer. That means if they like you and your service and feel it would be valuable to others, they are naturally inclined to recommend you to help the people they know.

When designing your campaign, you should choose a reward that is aligned with and relevant to your business. Use your creativity and come up with something fun and exciting. We recommend brainstorming the campaign and rewards with your team, staff, or referral partners. This creates more energy and brings life to the program.

If you run an office or have a staff of agents, sales consultants, or service technicians working for you, imagine what will happen once you develop a referral culture throughout your entire organization. If you involve everyone on your team in the program creation process, you will increase both buy-in and long-term participation by your team members. Especially when you track and reward them when they help drive in new referrals from your clients and customers or even their own personal social sphere.

Now, before we discuss recommendations for potential *Referral Rewards*, we have to give you a quick disclaimer. You MUST research and understand all regulatory restrictions your industry may have when it comes to rewarding people for referrals. While most industries have no state or federal regulations that prohibit you from offering rewards or incentives, there are some industries that completely prohibit or severely restrict the value of the gift or reward you can give. That's why it's always a good idea to check with your attorney regarding compensation restrictions that may apply to you. Your industry association should be able to provide you guidance on these matters as well.

Now that I've given you our official disclaimer and made our attorneys happy, let's explore some great incentives to rewards your *Referral Champions*.

Popular Referral Rewards:

1. Cash Rewards
2. Gift Certificates for your Services
    a. $25/ $50/ $100 Per Client or,
    b. 1 Free Visit/Treatment or,
    c. 1 Free Month/Year
3. Movie, Restaurant, or Starbucks Gift Cards
4. iPads, Tablets, and TVs
5. Tickets to Concerts or Sporting Events
6. Inclusion in Special Client Appreciation Parties
7. Weekend Getaways or Mini-Vacations
8. Related Products or Services Provided by your Referral Partners

Your goal is to get people excited about referring you, so they're constantly on the lookout scouting for your new clients. Of course, rewards that give away the products or services you provide are an easy and natural option. Plus, those who refer clients to you are already clients themselves and are more likely to use your service again anyway. That's why giving gift certificates for your service can help boost client loyalty. In addition, promoting your service as the reward gives you another opportunity to remind people about the services you offer.

How Much Should You Spend?

When deciding upon your *Referral Reward*, remember the money you invest in the campaign will be a fraction of the potential profit of all the new clients you are receiving. This is especially true when you consider the lifetime value of each new client.

When offering cash or gift certificates as rewards, you need to decide if you want to offer a flat fee reward, or a percentage of the purchases made. Both strategies work well, but your program should be aligned with your industry, business model, and brand.

For Example:

- **Refer 4 and It's Free** – this gives clients a 25% credit or discount for future purchases. Of course, not all clients will redeem these rewards, which will mean you will have no expense for some of the referrals you receive, and your clients still feel good that they received a reward even if they never redeem it. The downside of this type of reward is that the tracking and accounting can be cumbersome.
- **$25 / $50 / $100 Referral Reward** – this strategy is similar to the one we just discussed. The difference is that this allows you to give a physical gift certificate or gift card that clients can use in the future. People often feel more recognized and rewarded when receiving a physical gift in the mail. Plus, if a professional wins your contest or prize, it gives you a great reason to pop-by their place of business to deliver the prize in person and deepen your relationship.
- **10% Referral Reward**– this strategy is more of an affiliate model where you incentivize people who refer you by sharing the revenues you generate with them. This strategy can be highly successful but should be used withstrategic alliances and referral partners rather than clients,as some people may feel uncomfortable being paid for helping people they care about.

3. Promote Your Program

Now that you've decided upon the type of campaign and reward that is best for your business, it's time to start promoting it.

When creating your referral program, make it as easy as possible for people to refer clients to you. That's why we suggest you incorporate the following promotional strategies:

- **Print referral cards**: You can actually empower your clients with printed referral cards that give their friends discounts or special offers. Consider incorporating a discount or reward for your clients when they refer their friends, so both people have extra motivation to take advantage of your offer and use your services. Just be sure to train your staff to give these out to all of your clients and customers.
- **Give out gift certificates**: Giving gift certificates is another way you can empower your clients to spread the word about your business. If you decide to give out gift certificates, be sure to include a brochure on your products or services to make it easier for people to share why they love your business.
- **Post a sign in your place of business**: Print a sign you can display on your desk, wall, reception area, service bay, or other public areas. If you have salespeople or other employees who work for you, be sure to print these up for each person's desk or workspace, so you build buzz and maximize the results of your campaign.
- **Mail your best clients**: To announce your program, send out a personal letter or thank you card to each of your best clients. You may want to ask them for their help in referring their friends or simply thank them for their business and give them a way to help their loved ones. Either way, sending them a friendly letter personally signed by you along with gift certificates or referral cards they can give to their friends can help boost your business quickly.

- **Incorporate throughout your business**: Another easy way to promote your new *Referral Rewards* program is to incorporate your offer into your invoices, receipts, and other statements. Look at each and every printed
- or electronic communication you send to your clients throughout your client engagement cycle and look for ways to promote your program. You can also include your referral cards or gift certificates in anything you mail, ship, or deliver to your clients. That way, you are automatically asking for referrals without ever having to ask yourself.
- **Call your best client:** You should also consider calling your most pleasurable or profitable clients and letting them know you want to do something special for them. By making a personal call, you deepen your relationship and create an opportunity for your clients to give you referrals immediately during your call.
- **Create a video:** Shoot a quick 1 or 2-minute video giving the details of your *Referral Rewards* campaign. Post the video on YouTube and include a link on your website, newsletter, and all your social media sites.
- **Email your sphere:** Once you are ready to promote your program, be sure to email your database of customers and prospects with details about your referral campaign or contest. You may even want to include a private to a special offer page that is exclusively available to friends and family of your best clients. This helps people feel special and increase the likelihood they will pass on your promotion to their family and friends.
- **Go social:** Promote your campaign or contest on your social media sites and fan pages, including Facebook, LinkedIn, Google+, Instagram, and Twitter.

You can share the *Referral Reward* you are offering to incentivize your social sphere to spread the word. This helps expand your reach beyond your current client base to maximize the awareness for your campaign.

- **Promote on your website:** Be sure to include an announcement on the homepage of your website along with your blogs. Remember to give people plenty of reasons to spread the word and include links to your special offer and appointment or calendar link.
- **Announce in your newsletter:** Include a *Referral Rewards* section in your printed or electronic newsletter. Since you are already promoting your business and educating your clients, newsletters give you a natural opportunity to ask for referrals and promote the rewards you are offering to those who do. As we will discuss in the next section, you should also recognize and thank referring clients.
- **Promote with your partners**: To increase the total exposure of your campaign, we recommend including your referral partners. You can either design the program jointly with some of your best partners or simply give them referral cards or gift certificates they can give to their clients. This helps them feel good because it helps them increase their perceived value with their clients. This also enrolls them with an easy means of recommending you when the opportunity presents itself.

When creating your campaign promotion, remember to:

- **Use photos showing your rewards:** An attractive photo of the reward you are offering will help build buzz and entice people to refer you. If you're giving away a gift certificate or gift card, be sure to print the value of the gift card in text over the photo showing the product or service people will receive.

- **Include entry and reward/prize info:** If you are holding a referral contest, be sure to give detailed descriptions of your prize as well as a description of how people earn entries in your contest. Be sure to include all of the rules or restrictions of your campaign. If you are promoting your contest online, include a link to a rules page or list them on the bottom of your Referral Rewards page.
- **Include share buttons and social media links:** This makes it easy for people to recommend you to their friends and social sphere. If you are promoting your program online, you want to take advantage of the network reach of social media by incorporating a share button on your website,

Instagram, or Facebook page. You may also want to give your clients suggestions of how they can best recommend you to other people.

Always Be Promoting

However you choose to promote your *Referral Rewards* program, the key to your success will be the amount of promotion you do. In our age of information overload, attention spans have never been shorter. If you send out a single email, post, or tweet about your program, that won't be enough to keep people engaged with your program. You don't want to annoy your clients, but you should send subtle reminders periodically to keep your *Referral Rewards* program top of mind. Consistency is the key.

Whatever method you choose, remember that effective promotion of your customer referral program is an ongoing process. If you want your program to be successful, you need to remind people about it from time to time. Keep people engaged with your program through regular emails and social posts online, and not only will you bring in new customers but also more passionate fans that compound your referrals exponentially.

4. Recognize and Reward Referrers

Throughout your *Referral Rewards* campaign, you should be recognizing and rewarding anyone who refers others to you. This is actually the best way to continually promote your program. Not only will you show your clients how grateful you are for their referrals, but you are also triggering their ego-based need for public recognition. As you illustrate examples of clients who are referring their friends, you build social proof and help others feel more comfortable and more likely to refer you.

You can use each of the promotional strategies we covered in the last section to promote your top referrers. You may even want to create a referral leader board where you prominently recognize people who are referring new business. Again, this helps ensure your entire team or organization is active in the *Referral Rewards* campaign and conversation.

If you are holding a referral contest, be sure to recognize referrers throughout your contest. This helps build buzz and keeps the campaign alive. At the conclusion of your referral contest, be sure to publicly recognize the winner(s).

For optimal results, we recommend that you:

- Shoot a video or go live on social media showing the drawing of the winning name to create excitement and show the drawing Is being held fairly.
- Send an email to your email list congratulating the winner(s). We recommend you list the names of every single person who referred new clients to you as they will appreciate the recognition. This is often a stronger motivator than any prize you may offer. Be sure to include your referral partners as this is a great opportunity to promote them and their business to your client base.
- Post on all of your websites, social media sites, andfan pages to get extra mileage out of the campaign.
- Ask the winner to give you a shout-out on their social media pages and create a quick thank you video.
- Email contestants offering them an alternative prize which may be a gift certificate or discount on your services.
- Meet with the winner to give them their prize in person. Take a photo or video showing the client receiving their prize. This will allow you to promote it in your office, on your website, social media, and in other client communications.

- If your services are part of the prize, capture the winner's testimonial and ask them for referrals to people who fit your ideal client profile. Video is best because you can transcribe it and use it in print as well.

Following these steps will help you create a powerful and profitable referral contest. Once your contest ends, consider promoting another contest or event to keep the momentum building and to prime clients for future campaigns.

As you can see, creating a *Referral Rewards* campaign can create tremendous word-of-mouth recommendations and referrals for your business. By incorporating these practices into your business, you create a culture of referrals quickly and easily. Doing so will help you eliminate your high-cost marketing activities while providing you with a steady stream of profitable and pleasurable clients.

Here are some examples showing how some people recognize their referral contest winners:

While the best way to motivate is to compensate, recognizing and rewarding your Referral Champions can boost your business quickly. Get people scouting business for you by scanning this QR code or visiting the following link:

https://ravingreferrals.com/reward

CHAPTER 8

Master the Art of the Ask

The number one reason some professionals receive more referrals than others is that they simply ask for them. Many people feel uncomfortable and awkward asking their clients for referrals. However, once you are prepared and you have a strategy for when and how to ask, it will feel natural and comfortable for both you and the other party.

In their book *Selling Professional Services*, Chuck and Evan Polin write,

> *"Most professionals do not ask for referrals because they are afraid they have nothing to offer in return. They are often surprised when they discover that the referring party's only expectation is that their client or friend receive the best service. When you ask for referrals, the other party typically expects less in return than you would think."*

Set the Stage

While most people ask for referrals once they have finished serving their clients, we recommend having a conversation about referrals and introductions at the end of your first client meeting. This sets the stage for a referral conversation later in your client service cycle.

Earl Kemper is a referral master and has been recognized as the #1 coach for ActionCOACH five times for the Americas region and twice globally. Earl is truly skilled at helping companies grow and create predictable profitability. A cornerstone of Earl's system is the ability to grow the business by systemizing their referrals.

Earl primarily coaches top-producing financial advisors helping them dramatically increase assets under management. He teaches them to weave a pre-referral request into every new client conversation saying:

> *"Thanks so much for meeting with me today. Before you leave, I'd like to ask for your help. As you may know, I am in the process of expanding my business, and one of the ways I keep my costs down is by working primarily by referral, so I don't have to spend much time or money on advertising. Once I've taken care of you and hopefully have exceeded your expectations, I'd like to ask your permission to ask you for referrals. Would that be all right?"*

You'll find people are extremely receptive to this question because everyone likes to help other people. Also, you haven't asked them for a referral at that moment in time. You've simply gotten their permission to ask them for referrals and introductions in the future once you've provided your services and earned their trust.

Listen for Referral Triggers

After your client has given their approval to ask for referrals and introductions in the future, you need to be on the lookout for expressions of appreciation. These *Referral Triggers* let you know when it's time to ask for a referral or introduction because your clients are in peak referral state.

Listen closely, and whenever your clients say any of these *Referral Triggers*, it's time to ask for referrals:

- Thank you so much!
- You are so good at what you do!
- You did a great job!
- I couldn't have done it without you!
- You're the best!
- This is beautiful!
- Wow, I love it!
- I can't believe how much I saved!
- I can't believe how much I made!
- You've helped me save so much time/energy/money!
- I look/feel great!
- I have a friend/neighbor/client who might need your services.
- I should introduce you to…

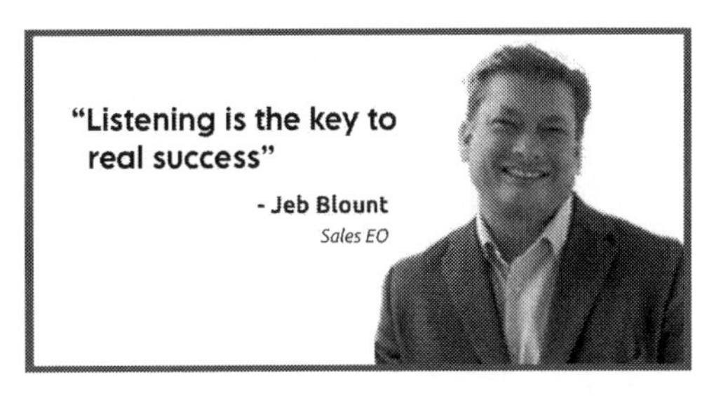

When you hear any of these *Referral Triggers*, immediately smile and say,

> *"I'm so glad you feel that way. I love helping clients like you {share your Service Statement}. By the way, I may have mentioned before that I am expanding my business, so if you know any {describe your Perfect Prospect} who might need help {share your Service Statement}, I'd love to connect with them and see if I can help them the way I helped you.*
>
> *Do you know anyone right now who is looking to {share your Service Statement}?"*

Be ready to ask for referrals when opportunities arise and when trust has been established in the relationship. Actively listen for the *Referral Triggers* and be prepared to deliver your *ask* confidently and naturally.

Never miss a prime opportunity to ask. Even if they don't have a referral for you now, you've planted a seed and set the stage so they refer you later when they hear of someone that might benefit from your services.

What you'll find is that when people voluntarily express their appreciation for your work, they are much more likely to introduce you to others who need your services. Plus, you get the added benefit of your perfect prospects hearing a passionate testimonial about you and the services you provide.

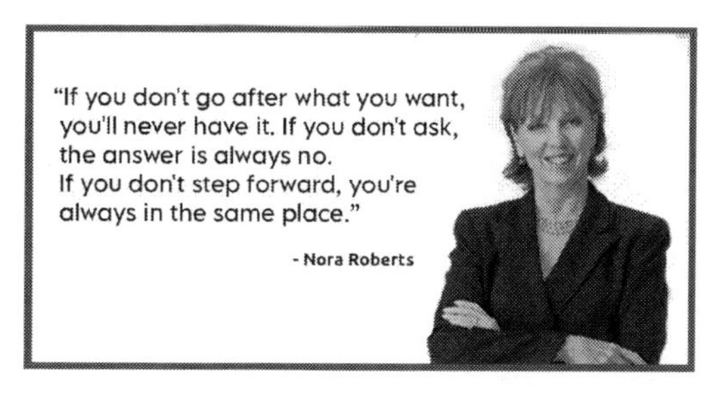

A-S-K to G-E-T

One of the greatest lessons I've learned from Mark Victor Hansen is to A-S-K to G-E-T. If you've never read his book with Jack Canfield called, *The Aladdin Factor*, take a moment and order it now either in printed form, eBook, or as an audiobook. The key concept of the book is that the more you ask for what you want, the more you will get it. If you are in sales, are self-employed, or make a living selling products or services, the more often you ask for the sale.

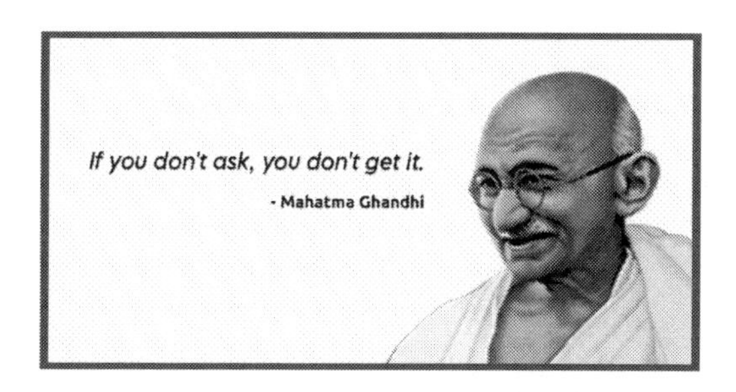

The beauty is, we're going to teach you how to generate referrals and introductions simply by asking questions that lead people to the *Referral Triggers* we just described. By asking clients questions about their satisfaction with your products or services, you set the stage for an expression of appreciation which often leads to opportunities to ask for referrals.

When meeting with your clients, try inserting the following questions into the conversation:

- I hope you're pleased with the service I've provided. Is there anything I can do to make you even happier?
- Now that we've been working together for a while, I'm wondering if you can tell me what you have found most valuable about working with me?
- I'm committed to growing my business through exceptional service. On a scale of 1-10, how happy would you say you are with my services? What would make it a 10?
- Do you mind if I ask what you have liked best about working with me?
- If you don't mind me asking, if you knew someone who was looking for a {insert your profession} how likely would you be to recommend me? What would you say?

If the client responds positively, you can follow up by saying,

> *"I'm so glad to hear that. I hope you'll recommend me any time you hear any {describe your perfect prospect} mention that they are looking for a good {insert your profession} or need help {share your Service Statement}. Is there anyone who comes to mind who might need my help?"*

Not only will these questions lead to more referrals, but they will also give you testimonials you can use to market your services. Just be sure to capture what they say and ask for permission to use their testimonial on your website and promotional materials.

Another way for you to comfortably ask for referrals is by saying:

> *"By the way, if you ever have a friend or family member you think might benefit from my services, I would be happy to meet with them for free to see how I might be able to help them."*

Ideally, you should describe your *Perfect Prospect Profile* and *Service Statement*, so they know exactly what type of clients you are looking to serve and how you help them. You might simply say that one of your specialties is working with recent retirees, first-time home buyers or whatever describes your perfect prospect and ideal client. Adding this detail into the conversation gives them clarity so they will be on the lookout for clients they can refer you.

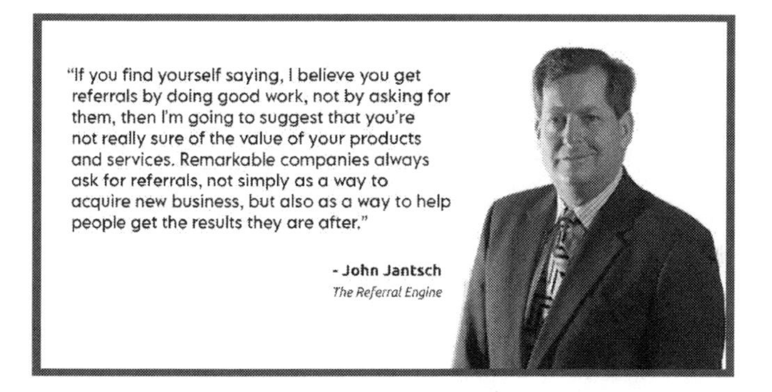

Referral Offers and Discounts

Another way you can comfortably ask for referrals and introductions is by letting clients know you offer special services, offers, or discounts for referred clients. If this applies to your business, you might say something like:

> *"As you may know, I prefer working with people who are referred to us. Right now, we're giving a special discount to friends or family of our existing clients. If there's anyone*

> *you'd like to refer, they will get an extra 20% off our premier package (customize with your offer). And, of course, I'll take extra special care of them since they're coming from you. Is there anyone you can think of who might like to take advantage of this?"*

For optimal results, we suggest creating and giving them a refer-a-friend gift certificate they can quickly and easily hand out to people when they talk about your services. This gives prospective clients an overview of your services, along with a testimonial from someone they trust.

As you start integrating these conversations into your client dialogues, you will find people are happy to refer others when asked at the right time and in the right way.

Practice and Perfect

While you've probably spent thousands of hours practicing and perfecting your trade or profession, you most likely haven't spent much time learning and practicing how to attract referrals and introductions. Since practice makes perfect, we recommend you partner with another professional and roll-play these conversations, so they become second nature to you both.

As you master the art of the ask, you will find that clients refer you without even being asked as you build a business that is powered by referrals. In addition to asking for referrals, start asking for anything and everything you want in life.

- Ask for an appointment
- Ask for an introduction
- Ask to take the next step
- Ask if they would like a demo

- Ask if you can give them a tour
- Ask for the contract
- Ask when they would like to get started
- Ask if they would like to move forward

Asking for what you want dramatically increases the likelihood that you will get it. Best of all, you have nothing to lose because if the answer is no, you are in the exact same position you were before you asked. If they say yes, you will have achieved your desired outcome and have moved your business forward.

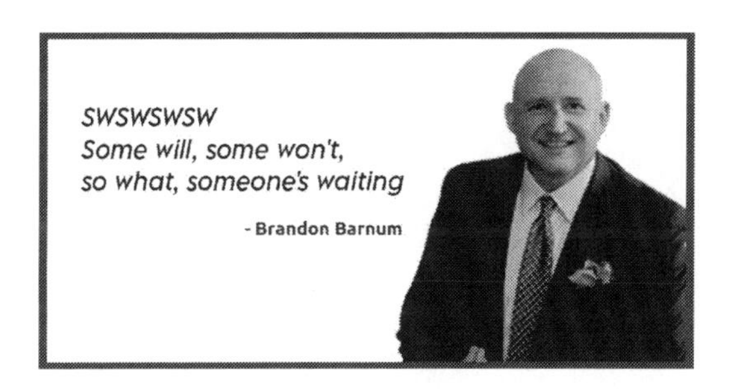

Mastering the Art of the Ask is one of the top practices that create more success. Scan the QR code or visit the link below for a quick video message on how to A-S-K and G-E-T. While we're on the subject, we're asking you to share this video with your network. Together, we can help them get clear on what they are asking for in their personal and professional lives:

RavingReferrals.com/ask

CHAPTER 9

Client Appreciation Events

Back in 1999, I learned the value of client appreciation parties from a Realtor named Mikalan Moiso. Each year, she held her annual New Year's Eve party at a swanky downtown hotel in Portland, Oregon. It was the event of the year, and in order to get an invitation to the black-tie event, you simply had to give Mikalan at least one good referral throughout the course of the year.

My wife and I will never forget ringing in the new millennium of 2000 playing poker, listening to the Frank Sinatra crooner, and tasting delicious eats and treats.

Months after the event, I asked Mikalan how impactful the event was on her business. I was shocked to hear that her annual event is the single biggest source of clients for her. In fact, she had shifted the vast majority of her annual marketing budget to the event because her clients and social sphere wanted to make sure they gave her referrals so they received their golden ticket to the event. The event was so successful, it led to Mikalan being named the 2004 Portland Metropolitan Association of Realtors® Broker of the Year.

After learning this strategy from her, I went on to host several client appreciation events, including private concerts, movie showings, wine tastings, holiday parties, and charity events.

Everyone loves a great party. That's why a great way to show your clients and customers how much they mean to your business is to throw a customer appreciation party. A client event can be an impactful way to celebrate your customers, recognize milestones, and say "thank-you" for all the business they have done with you and your company. Not only will you bring clients together for a fun and festive event, but you also create a culture of community that unites your team as you create an evening your clients will never forget.

- **Art Showings** – Partner with an art gallery and host a private showing.
- **Awards Parties** – Invite your clients to a hotel, bar, restaurant, or private theater to watch the Oscars, Grammys, Golden Globes, or other awards show.
- **Bowling Parties** – Rent an entire bowling alley or just a few lanes and give prizes for the bowlers who get the most strikes or spares as well as the top individual and team scores.
- **Casino Night** – Hire a party company to bring casino tables and dealers giving out chips and awarding prizes for the top chip stacks.
- **Charity Fundraising Events** – Create your own event or buy a table at a fundraising dinner inviting your top clients.
- **Cigar Night** – Host a party featuring cigars and whiskey tasting for your high-action clients.
- **Concerts** – Buy tickets for your VIP clients to an upcoming concert or host a private party with an 80s cover band or local musician.
- **Cornhole Tournaments** – Host a cornhole tournament inviting top clients to register their own teams.
- **Golf Tournaments** – Produce your own golf tournament or simply buy a foursome and invite VIPs to join you on the greens.

- **Holiday Parties** – Throw a private party for Valentine's Day, Independence Day, Halloween, Thanksgiving, Christmas, or New Year's Eve.
- **Private Movie Showings** – Rent out a theater and have your own private showing of the latest blockbuster film.
- **Sports Events** – Host a tailgate party, rent a private box, or simply buy tickets and invite your best clients and customers for a sporting event.
- **TopGolf Tournaments** – Rent a few private bays at TopGolf and give prizes for top scores.
- **Wine Tours and Tastings** – Host a private party at a winery or tasting room.

Become a Charity Champion

Of all the events and campaigns that I've used over the years, the most fulfilling and rewarding have been charity events. In my opinion, one of the absolute best ways to build goodwill with your clients and customers is to support charities and causes you are passionate about.

Cause-related marketing has evolved from a short-term tactic used to spike sales into a powerful positioning discipline used to build brand equity and elevate corporate perception. It's not only good for the community; it's good for business.

The Results Are In

There have been numerous research studies over the years that prove consumers want to know about the impact your company makes in their community and in the world. The more you communicate what you are doing to make a difference, the more loyalty you win with your clients and customers.

Just take a look at what research companies have learned after surveying Americans nationwide:

- 83% of U.S. consumers want more of the products and services they use to benefit causes (*2010 Cone Cause Evolution Study).*
- 80% said they'd be "likely to switch brands, about equal in price and quality, to one that supports a cause" (*2010 Cone Cause Evolution Study).*
- 93% of consumers want to know what companies are doing to make the world a better place (*2011 Cone/Echo Global CR Study).*
- 66% of people believe it's no longer enough for corporations to merely give money away, but that they must integrate good causes into their day-to-day business (*2009 Edelman good purpose Consumer Study).*
- 90% of consumers want companies to tell them the ways they are supporting causes (*2010 Cone Cause Evolution Study).*

While this research is a few years old, we believe this is a trend that will continue to grow. Especially with Millennials and Generation Z having been raised in this new era of corporate responsibility and social impact. Bottom line, the more you show you care, the more you inspire your community to care about you and your company. So, choose a charity or cause that you are passionate about that is in alignment with your brand and your community. Get involved and design ways that your company and your community can make a difference – together.

The Ultimate Wishman

One of the favorite people I've had the pleasure of meeting was Frank Shankwitz, co-founder of the Make-A-Wish Foundation. Changing lives and granting wishes is what Frank dedicated his life to. If you haven't seen the movie *Wishman* about Frank's life, you owe it to yourself to watch this heartwarming film. You'll be glad you did.

While serving as an Arizona Highway Patrol officer, Frank had the honor of granting a wish for a 7-year-old boy named Chris who was battling leukemia. Turned out this boy had a dream of being a Highway Patrol Motorcycle Officer like his heroes, Ponch and John, from the television show, "CHiPs". After hearing of Chris' desire, Frank and a few of his fellow officers sprang into action and made Chris' dream come true. They had a uniform custom-crafted for Chris and gave him an old police badge and a "Smokey Bear" hat so he would feel like a real cop. Frank even set up a special course so Chris could drive a battery-powered motorcycle and qualify for the officer's wings he so deeply desired. A few short days later, Chris' body gave up the fight, and on May 3, 1980, he passed away.

This event led Frank to found Make-A-Wish to grant wishes for other sick children. Not long ago, I asked Frank what helped the charity become the global force for the good that it is today. Frank's answer was simple and powerful, "Disneyland." Turns out the first official wish the start-up charity granted was taking 7-year-old Frank 'Bopsy' Salazar to Disneyland.

This powerful partnership created massive visibility for both organizations and inspired millions of people to donate and do more for others in need. What started as a simple way to help a dying boy fulfill his wish, has led to over 450,000 children having their dreams fulfilled.

Over the years, Disney has invested millions of dollars promoting the impact they have made by granting wishes for Make-A-Wish kids. Every time a mom watches a commercial or story of a dying child's wish being fulfilled at Disneyland, it boosts loyalty and wins Disney another fan of the brand.

Starting Small Makes a Big Difference

The good news is that you don't have to create your own charity to tap into the power of cause-related marketing. You can simply raise awareness, funds, and support for great causes and charities already doing good work.

If you're curious how I got started as a *Charity Champion*, you're going to love the next chapter.

Everyone loves to have fun. That's why client appreciation events are a great way to recognize and reward your best clients and referral partners. Scan this QR code or visit the link below for a quick video message on how to grow your business celebrating your community:

https://ravingreferrals.com/celebrate/

CHAPTER 10

Referral of a Lifetime

My favorite referral of all time was to Mark Victor Hansen, co-author of the best-selling book series *Chicken Soup for the Soul.* Mark is an amazing man who has appeared on *Oprah*, CNN, and *The Today Show*, as well as in *Time Magazine, U.S. News & World Report, USA Today, The New York Times*, and *Entrepreneur Magazine.*

Among Mark's many achievements is his Guinness book world record for selling the most non-fiction books in the history of the world, with over 500 million books sold. That's a staggering number that still blows my mind.

I was referred to Mark by one of his closest friends back in 2004 when I was serving as a volunteer on the Corporate Industry Council for the charity Northwest Medical Teams, which has since rebranded to Medical Teams International (MedicalTeams.org). This faith-based charity provides emergency medical relief in response to floods, famine, and other natural disasters.

I got involved after hearing one of their volunteer doctors share his story of taking what I call a voluntour trip over to Africa. The doctor recounted his story of 18-hour days spent caring for countless patients. No matter how many patients he treated, each day ended with a mother chasing the van crying, *"What about my child?"* The doctor's heartbreaking story stirred my heart into action, so I accepted the invitation and started raising money and awareness for the work they were doing.

The Perfect Choice

The biggest fundraiser of the year for Northwest Medical Teams was their annual *Spirit of Life Awards,* where they would honor a local titan of business for their impact on the community. Knowing I was a fan of personal development training, I was asked to help secure the featured speaker for the luncheon. Having just read, *The One Minute Millionaire, The Enlightened Way to Wealth* by Mark Victor Hansen and Robert Allen, I knew their message of doing well while doing good would be a perfect fit for this audience and might encourage the attendees to give more.

As fortune would have it, a financial advisor friend named Al Sizer had known Mark for over 30 years. It turns out Mark and Al came up together on the public speaking circuit back in the 1970s and had built a special friendship forged over three decades of traveling together and speaking at the same events.

After working up the courage to ask Al to ask Mark to speak at the event, I was beyond excited when Al called back, saying Mark's calendar was available that day and he was interested in helping.

After learning Mark's speaking fee, it was clear the charity couldn't afford him. After all, any fee NW Med paid would reduce the total impact the charity made, which was the entire reason for the event. That's when I made the courageous step of committing to cover Mark's speaker fee myself. Fortune favors the bold, so I gave my financial commitment and took a deep breath of faith, knowing that paying it forward always has a high ROI.

Two for the Price of One

What happened next was amazing. When coordinating the details with Mary, Mark's Vice President, she was so inspired by the cause we were supporting that she generously offered to have Mark speak in the evening at no additional cost in addition to the lunch event. This meant we were able to put on two events while he was in town.

Again, I said YES and quickly went to work producing an additional evening event we called "Success with Integrity," with my company, Integrity Lending, as the event's premier sponsor. This empowered my loan officers to invite their top clients and referral partners to join us for this fun, feel-good, celebrity event. I have to tell you, the pride and unity this event brought to my team was immeasurable and was celebrated for months.

The morning of May 18, 2004, I had the honor of joining Mark Victor Hansen and Al Sizer for breakfast, along with three representatives of NW Med, including the CEO and the Chairman of the board, as well as the development director I had been working with for months.

During our breakfast, Mark asked about my companies and nonchalantly shared, *"I can easily refer you a billion dollars in commercial loans,"* at which point quick calculations of the commissions and income that represented flashed through my head. That was the moment it hit me just how influential this man was and how impactful his endorsement could be for both my companies and me personally.

Throughout the two events of that day, Mark inspired and entertained over 500 people, helping us raise donations that delivered over $1.2 million worth of medical aid and supplies to those in need. As you can imagine, it was a day I will never forget.

As he closed his final presentation of the night, Mark made an offer for those who wanted to learn more. I immediately went to the back of the room and bought every CD and book he had for sale, including *Dreams Don't Have Deadlines, The Power of Focus,* and *The Aladdin Factor – How to Ask for and Get Anything You Want.*

The following week, as my wife and I traveled to Maui, I spent much of the trip listening to Mark mentor me through his audios. Mark's masterful training expanded my thinking and helped me reframe what was possible for my life.

During each of Mark's talks, he challenged the audience to make a list of 101 goals, including the date each person planned to achieve each goal they set. Since my wife goes to bed early, I spent hours every night on the beach under the stars dreaming of all I hoped to achieve over my lifetime. By the end, I had created hundreds of short and long-term goals.

One of my top ambitions was to enroll Mark Victor Hansen to become my personal mentor. After returning from Maui, I gathered my nerve and made what felt like the scariest call I had ever made, asking Mark to be my personal mentor. He graciously agreed and has impacted my life in countless ways since I stepped out in faith and asked for what I wanted.

Mark had no idea, but one of the goals I wrote on that beach was, *"To have Mark Victor Hansen write about me in a book by May 28, 2005."* A few months after writing down that goal, Mark called and said, *"Robert Allen and I are writing our follow-up to The One Minute Millionaire which will be called Cracking the Millionaire Code. We'd like to feature you in the book. Would you be okay with that?"*

Excitedly, I said *"YES,"* and almost as if by divine design, *Cracking the Millionaire Code* was published on May 31, 2005.

Dreams Fulfilled

Within 12 months of following Mark's system and writing down my goals, I had traveled to Asia, Europe, Africa, and South America for business. These were foreign lands I had only dreamt of traveling to before soaking in Mark's mentorship.

Before meeting Mark, the largest transaction I had been involved with was a $10 million development loan. Now, I was working on international financings of $200 million. Twenty times larger than any transaction I had been involved in before Mark telling the world about me!

You can just imagine the clients and opportunities that the book brought because of the credibility and social proof of Mark's endorsement and promotion. When a celebrity or company with massive authority and influence endorses a nd promotes you, it creates tremendous credibility that unlocks lucrative opportunities.

Within weeks of writing out my goals, Mark invited me to be a VIP guest of his MEGA Book Marketing, MEGA Info-Marketing, and MEGA Speaking Empire conferences. He routinely had me stand and introduce myself and share how I could help the audience. He later asked me to teach finance to his Enlightened Millionaire Institute Inner Circle both in the U.S. and abroad.

Around the World in 30 Days

That book became a turning point in my career, not only because of the business opportunities that came from readers of the book, but more importantly because the experience was powerful proof of our human ability to create and manifest anything we want. The key is to get clear on exactly what we want to achieve, accomplish, or experience.

Of the 338 goals I wrote on that beach, over 100 were achieved in the first 12 months alone, a few of which included:

- Enroll Mark Victor Hansen as my personal mentor by 7/7/2004
- Have Mark Victor Hansen write about me in a book published by 5/28/2005
- Have Mark Victor Hansen invite me to his private home in Kona, Hawaii, by 5/28/2005
- Start a 501(c)3 charity by 5/28/2005
- Travel to New York City, London, Hong Kong, China, and Africa by 5/28/2005
- Hike the Great Wall of China by 5/28/2005
- Meet U2's lead singer Bono by 5/28/2005

Prior to meeting Mark, I had barely left the country. Within one year of his mentoring, I took a 30-day around-the-world trip Eastward from Portland, Oregon to London, then off to Hong Kong, Macau, and Guangzhou, China, before taking the final leg to Caracas, Venezuela and Bucaramunga, Colombia.

As I met new clients and prospective partners, I gave them a copy of the *Cracking the Millionaire Code* book with my business card inserted on the page that started featuring my personal, professional, and charitable pursuits. That book elevated my status with my clients, team, and referral partners while simultaneously attracting new clients from around the world – just as Mark had predicted.

Mark taught me the power of specificity in goal setting, including writing down the exact date you plan to achieve each goal. In case you missed it, *Cracking the Millionaire Code* was published three days after the goal date I had typed on my laptop less than one year prior, a fact that astounds me to this day.

My purpose in sharing this story with you is two-fold.

First, I want you to truly understand that you can create anything you want in your life when you get clear, put it in writing, and commit yourself to achieve your desire or dream. You will have to take massive action and ask others to assist you, but you can quickly transform your life simply by transforming your thinking.

Second, I hope to give you a vision for the power of getting endorsed, recommended, and promoted by people and companies that have the ability to take your business to an entirely new level. The key takeaway here is that just one key referral partner can transform your business and your life.

You just have to A-S-K to G-E-T.

Getting clear on what you want to achieve and experience is the foundation of success. Scan this QR code or visit the link below for an inspiring lesson on setting the goals that matter most to your future success:

https://ravingreferrals.com/mvh/

CHAPTER 11

Wealth Through Workshops

After meeting and being mentored by Mark Victor Hansen, one of the most important lessons he taught me was the power of producing events. There's simply no faster or more effective way to boost your expert status than educating audiences in person or online.

If you're a service professional, holding educational workshops is one of the best ways to win new clients. Events help you attract highly profitable prospects and establish yourself as a credible expert, which, in turn, will help you convert more clients at higher conversion rates.

The key is to fill your workshops with as many of your perfect prospects as possible so that you maximize the revenue you generate for your business.

When it comes to holding educational events, quality trumps quantity every time. It is better to teach a class to 10 business owners who match your *Perfect Prospect Profile* than to have 100 unqualified people in your audience. Be sure your event invitations and promotions are targeted to appeal to your ideal clients and perfect prospects.

7 Super Strategies to Fill Your Events with Perfect Prospects

The following seven time-tested and proven strategies will help you fill your next event with quality candidates for your services:

1. Invite Your Social Sphere

The best way to fill your events is with your own clients. They are the most likely to use your services again! In addition to your clients, you should also promote your upcoming events to both your personal and professional databases. Since these people already know, like, and trust you, they are likely to recommend your event once you have asked for their help and identified who the event will be most helpful for. If you charge for your events, you may want to offer a few gift guest passes people can give to their friends, clients, and colleagues. Just be sure to identify your perfect prospect profile, so they invite the right type of people to your event.

Here are a few ways you can invite hundreds of prospects in a matter of minutes:

- Email flyers and invitations to family, friends, and people in your clubs, churches, or charities
- Post events in your social network through Facebook, Twitter, Google+, and LinkedIn
- Email links to your training videos and post the links on your website, blog, and social sites
- Send LinkedIn messages to each of your current contacts inviting them to attend your event
- You can also print up and mail or hand out tickets to your next event, so people have something physical in hand which increases the perceived value of the event.

The key is to spread the word far and wide with people who are most likely to attend and invite others.

2. Develop Promotional Partnerships

Another great strategy that helps leverage the recommendations of others is to partner with businesses, charities, and associations that already serve your ideal clients. By offering to teach a class or give guest passes to your workshop as a gift to their clients, customers, members, and social media followers, you give them a high-perceived value item they can provide at no or low cost. Simply ask about the biggest challenges their stakeholders face and offer training that solves those challenges. The more you help them win customer loyalty, the more passionately they will promote your events.

We will cover this in detail in Chapter 17 on cross-promoting with your partners.

3. Invite Your Clients to Invite Their Clients

There's no disputing the power of a personal recommendation. That's why one of the best ways to fill your seminars and workshops is to have your current or past clients invite their customers, clients, employees, and strategic alliances to attend your event. After all, as they share their personal story of the impact you and your training have had on their business, their contacts will be much more inclined to attend your events and to use your services afterward.

This is especially powerful if you serve businesses or business owners since they will likely have a large database of your ideal clients. Just call up your best clients and let them know you've been thinking about their business. You can go on to explain that you have an idea you think will help them better serve their current clients and attract more clients at no cost to them. At that point, you've captured their attention and interest. Then you can walk them through your idea of providing exclusive training for their clients and prospects. You can even have them participate as a partner/sponsor for your upcoming workshop.

4. Co-Produce Events with Others

One of the most effective ways to promote your event to a larger audience is to co-produce seminars or workshops with other businesses or professionals who are looking to attract the same ideal client profile. For example, suppose you are holding a profit maximization workshop for business owners. In that case, you might consider partnering with CPAs, attorneys, financial advisors, banks, or commercial insurance brokers who serve the B2B market. If your prospects are home buyers, consider putting on a first-time homebuyer or real estate investment workshop and partnering with realtors, mortgage professionals, home inspectors, and contractors.

By partnering and sharing the costs of promoting and producing your seminar or workshop, you help other businesses gain access to new prospects at a reduced marketing expense for everyone. Plus, as your partners get new clients from the event, they will refer them back to you since you are the reason they won the business to begin with. This strategy also allows you to highly target your marketing while positioning you as the trusted expert and increasing your perceived credibility and expertise to a wider audience.

5. Speak at Other Events

There are numerous organizations that serve your ideal clients and are constantly looking for interesting speakers for their meetings and events. You gain tremendous credibility and visibility by volunteering to speak at events held by local Chambers of Commerce, banks, universities, the SBA, networking groups, and trade shows. Nonprofit organizations and associations that support and serve your target market are also great opportunities to reach prospective clients.

Once you have established your expertise throughout your training, the audience will be much more interested in attending your future workshops. Just be sure to include a closing slide that promotes your services and upcoming events. In addition, consider handing out worksheets that include details on your future workshops and offer your training services to those in need of a speaker. After all, sometimes, you need to do some shameless self-promotion to grow your business.

Be sure you have a call to action at the end of your presentation, letting your audience know the next steps you want them to take to move forward with you. Doing this each time you speak or teach will help fill your calendar with speaking engagements and bring more attendees to your events and clients to your business.

6. Offer Referral Rewards

Another great way to spread the word and expand your audience is to incentivize others to fill your events. You may be familiar with affiliate programs where businesses pay commissions on referrals that lead to sales, but have you ever considered offering to pay bounties or commissions to salespeople or marketing companies who help fill your events?

This strategy is especially effective when engaging marketing consultants or sales professionals who are used to working on a pay-for-performance basis. After all, these people speak with your target market every day and can easily promote your workshops and services. Just be very specific about your perfect prospect profile, so they invite the right people who are most likely to do business with you. This strategy also works if you host online webinars as you can easily track attendees using a custom affiliate tracking code unique for each affiliate or promotional partner.

7. Outsource to Assistants or Interns

As a busy professional, one of your biggest challenges is most likely time management. That's why you should consider delegating your promotional activities to an assistant or intern. This will help you maximize higher profit activities that you enjoy more. By training an assistant to manage your promotional activities, you focus your valuable time meeting with profitable prospects and clients.

Just use the list we've given you and create a plan for them to execute for you. If you don't already have staff who can help promote your events, just reach out to a local employment agency to hire a temp who can make the calls for you.

You can also contact a university or business school in your area and let them know you'd like to off er an internship for their students. You can usually find some great talent in the school of marketing with young adults eager to build their resumes and hungry for their first real job. While many will agree to do an unpaid internship with you, you may want to pay them a minimal hourly rate or a set amount for the quarter, so they are amply motivated. You can also make the internship unpaid but give them a bonus based on the number of attendees they help attract or actual clients that you close from the event.

These seven powerful strategies can help you fi ll your events with profitable prospects for your business. These strategies will also help you attract top, trusted pros which we will cover in the next chapter.

Scan this QR code or visit the link below for a
video message about creating wealth through workshops:

https://ravingreferrals.com/workshops/

CHAPTER 12

Partner with Top Trusted Pros

When it comes to building a steady stream of *Raving Referrals*, one of the most underutilized and most effective strategies is to partner with other professionals who already serve your ideal clients. That's because businesses and professionals who are serving your perfect prospects consistently hear requests and opportunities for the services you provide. Plus, when a respected professional or business owner recommends you to their clients, customers, and contractors, it increases trust and accelerates revenue.

While a happy client may know three or four ideal clients for you, a professional in a complementary industry may have three or four referrals for you each week or even each day. As you build your relationship and help them understand how you can help the people they serve, they will refer a steady source of profitable prospects.

Your job is to help them see you and your service as the solution their clients and customers are looking for. Once they view you as a trusted solution helping them solve problems for their clients, they will refer you more often because you add value to both them and their customers.

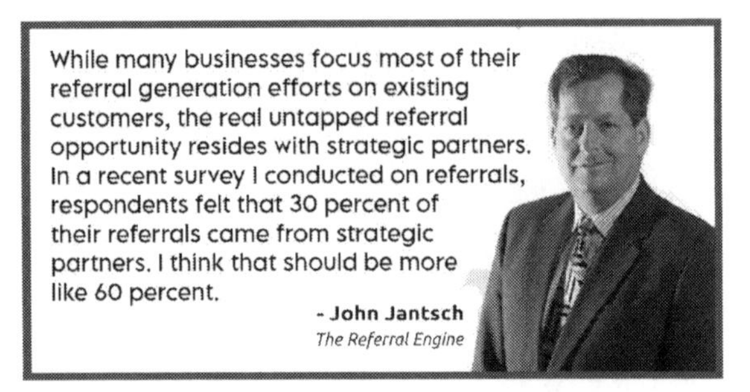

Over the past decade, we have surveyed thousands of business owners and professionals, asking them to identify how many referral partners they have who refer at least one new prospect every ninety days.

What has been surprising is that **32% of the professionals we surveyed said they had zero referral partners**. These people reported having to constantly scramble and hunt for new business because they had no one sending them profitable prospects. As a result, only half of the people in this group reported achieving an annual income of $50,000 or more.

The second group, which comprised **47% of total respondents, reported having one or two referral partners**. Although these people were getting a few referrals, they still found themselves in the bottom half of income earners in their companies or industries, with only 10% claiming to have achieved an annual income of $100,000 or more.

What was interesting was that the first two groups combined totaled 79% of everyone surveyed. Once again, the Pareto Principle (or 80/20 rule) proved to hold true.

The third group was made up of professionals who had three to nine referral partners, which equated to 19% of everyone surveyed. Over 70% of these people reported earning $100,000 or more per year, while under 20% of the first two groups achieved that income level.

Finally, the fourth group consisted of professionals claiming to have ten or more referral partners. What was shocking to our team was that only 2% of everyone who completed our survey was in this top group. Not surprisingly, this group reported much higher incomes, with all respondents claiming annual earnings over $100,000 and over half claiming annual income of more than $200,000 per year.

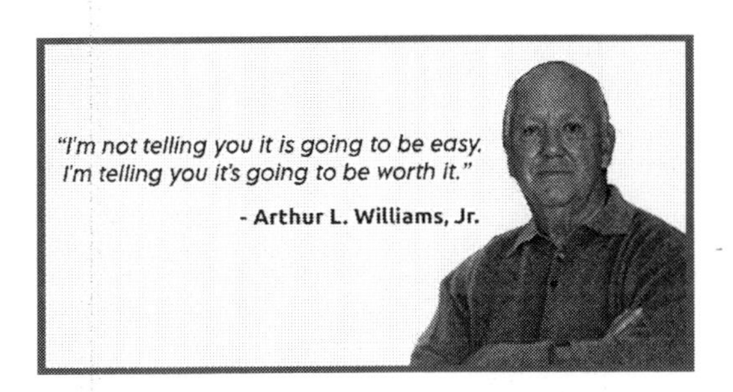

The Key to Success

I learned this strategy firsthand back in 1997 after starting as a mortgage loan officer. As I interviewed top producers in my firm and industry, I asked about their greatest source of business, and a common theme emerged.

All of the top producers I interviewed revealed that the bulk of their business came from a handful of professionals they had built referral partnerships with.

Without exception, their referral partners were all professionals who also served homeowners including Realtors, insurance agents, financial planners, accountants, and attorneys along with home services providers like contractors, home inspectors, and appraisers.

Makes sense, doesn't it? After all, every one of these people shared the same ideal clients. Plus, they often had customers asking about interest rates and for recommendations and introductions to a trusted mortgage lender.

Often, clients would share horror stories about their previous or current mortgage lender. Eager to solve their client's challenges, these professionals were thrilled to have a mortgage lender they could trust and to whom they could recommend their clients.

Best of all, since these professionals were highly trusted by their clients, they transferred that trust on to the lender they were referring to which created higher client conversion rates, higher profitability, and a better overall service experience.

Assemble Your Power Team

To create your Power Team of trusted professionals committed to doing business with you, start by identifying the top industries that already serve your ideal clients.

At HOA.com, we serve homeowners and are building the #1 Referral Network for Professionals Who Serve Homeowners. Our company is literally in the business of helping people build their own trusted network of vetted and certified professionals who also serve homeowners. By helping these professionals connect, collaborate, and cross-promote each other, we help them generate more business by helping the people we serve together.

The list below outlines professions by the clients they serve. If your clients are businesses or business owners, focus your attention on building partnerships with others who also serve home inspectors, appraisers, painters, plumbers, handymen, and contractors.

- Accountants
- Attorneys
- Bankers
- Business Coaches
- Carpet Cleaners
- Charities
- Chiropractors
- Cleaning Companies
- Credit Repair Experts
- Dentists
- Doctors
- Electricians
- Financial Advisors
- Garage Door Repair
- General Contractors
- Hair & Nail Salons
- Handymen
- Heating & AC Experts
- Insurance Agents
- Interior Designers
- Landscapers
- Locksmiths
- Marketing Consultants
- Massage Therapists
- Mobile IV Therapy
- Mortgage Pros
- Moving Companies
- New Home Builders
- Painters
- Personal Trainers
- Physical Therapists
- Photographers
- Pool Maintenance
- Plumbers
- Property Managers
- Real Estate Brokers
- Remodelers
- Restaurants
- Roofers
- Veterinarians
- Videographers
- Window & Door Experts

Your ideal referral partner list may look slightly different from these based on your industry and profession. That said, this should give you some great ideas on the types of professionals you should consider building strategic alliances with.

Envision your power team with your *Perfect Prospect* in the center of the hub surrounded by all of the other service providers they entrust their business to. If you serve consumers or homeowners, your Power Team might look like this:

While realtors were my primary source of mortgage clients, I also received *Raving Referrals* from accountants, attorneys, and financial advisors whose clients needed help buying or refinancing a home. Once I won their trust and wowed their clients, it was easy to keep the referrals flowing.

As you build your trusted team of referral partners, everyone will win more business together. In my case, I targeted remodelers because their clients usually needed financing. I helped the client refinance or get a home equity line of credit, which helped the remodeler get paid. A total win–win–win.

My network included everyone from home inspectors, appraisers, insurance agents, painters, plumbers, landscapers, pest control, and so many more. As I promoted each of these trusted pros on my website, blog, newsletters, and events, I won their loyalty and became their go-to mortgage lender.

So, the question is, who do you want on your trusted team?

Identify Your Ideal Partners

What industries do you want to build referral partnerships with? Review the proceeding list and write down the professions that can bring you the most business.

1. ____________	11. ____________
2. ____________	12. ____________
3. ____________	13. ____________
4. ____________	14. ____________
5. ____________	15. ____________
6. ____________	16. ____________
7. ____________	17. ____________
8. ____________	18. ____________
9. ____________	19. ____________
10. ____________	20. ____________

Prospective Partners

Most likely, you know several people in these professions you just listed. Perhaps you've known them for years or even decades and have never bothered to ask about doing business together. You may have family, friends, or other connections you've never pursued professionally. If that's true for you, I'm happy to tell you that you are sitting on an absolute goldmine.

What if you show them a win–win–win system where everyone prospers by working together?

As you help them understand who and how you help, many will gladly offer to promote you, especially when you approach professionals strategically, which we will cover shortly.

For each of the industries you've identified, start by asking yourself...

1. Who do I already know, like, and trust in that industry?
2. Who do I already refer business to?
3. Who in each industry already refers business to me?

Asking these three questions will help you create a targeted list of complementary professionals who already know, like, and trust you. Since trust accelerates relationships, starting with people you know will dramatically speed up your referrals and revenue.

The Proven Referral Partner Script:

Once you've identified your prospective partners, it's time to approach these professionals strategically. After twenty-plus years of testing, here's what we've found works best for creating profitable partnerships. If you follow this proven script below, you'll have people lining up to meet with you.

Just say…

> "Hi *(name)*, the reason I'm calling is that I'm creating a team of professionals I'll be recommending to all my clients. I was thinking about you because I have a lot of clients who could benefit from your services. I'd love to sit down with you to discuss the possibility of adding you to my team and promoting you. When's a good time to get together and strategize?"

Imagine receiving that call from someone you've known for years who serves your ideal clients all day long. Wouldn't you be excited about the possibility of having them consistently referring clients to you? Of course, you would! As long as they are someone you know, like, and trust.

When you follow this proven process, you can quickly create new referral partnerships with ease.

But how do you create partnerships with target professions when you don't know anyone in that field?

Great question. Glad you asked.

Filling Gaps

As you start creating strategic alliances and profitable partnerships, there will undoubtedly be some gaps. You may find a few industries or professions where you don't know anyone in that field. That's when asking clients to introduce you to top professionals they know, like, and trust is a powerful way to expand your team and your referral business.

Asking your VIP clients to introduce you to their top professional service providers gives you quick and easy access to high-quality professionals with whom it otherwise might be challenging to develop a relationship.

The good news is that asking clients for introductions is extremely easy when you know how. It also quickens your velocity to create profitable partnerships.

First, identify the profession to which you want to be introduced. Let's say you want to get connected with a quality CPA, for example. Just call up your client, or while sitting with them, simply say:

> *"Thanks so much for your time today. I'd like to ask for your help. As you may know, I am in the process of expanding my business, and I'm looking for a great CPA I can refer my clients to. I'm wondering if you know of any good CPAs you think I should meet. I'm planning to meet and interview two or three, and your CPA will be one of those I would like to meet with, not just for my personal business but also for the opportunity to refer clients to them. Is there anyone you'd recommend I meet with?"*

Once you ask, shut up and let them talk. It's normal to want to fill the space if they don't speak immediately but hold back and give them a few moments to think about who they can introduce you to. You will find most clients will be happy to help and introduce you to other professionals they use. Plus, since the introduction is coming from a mutual client, you already have something in common to start building rapport and trust with the other pro.

You can also post your request on social media. Not only will you increase the number of introductions you receive, but you will also let your clients and social sphere know they can turn to you and your team whenever they need help. You will be amazed to see top, trusted professionals reaching out to you proactively.

This strategy works extremely well because people love to help others. By giving them an opportunity to make an introduction, they are helping both you and the other professional they are introducing.

Ask for an Intro

WIN–WIN–WIN

Once your contact recommends someone for you to connect with, it's best to set the stage for the conversation. Just ask your contact to make an introduction and share the person's phone number so you can follow up proactively.

Simply say,

> "Thanks so much for the introduction. Would you be willing to make a quick call or send them a text to tell them how we know each other and that I will be calling them (*date and time of scheduled call*)?
>
> Is there anything you think I should know before I call them?"

Using this approach, the person to whom you are being introduced will be expecting and even looking forward to your call... all before you even dial their digits.

Once you've been introduced, simply call the professional at the appointed time, mention your client's name, and share that they come highly recommended by your mutual client. This creates instant connection and is the common ground that opens the door and fast-tracks a mutually prosperous partnership.

By reaching out to professionals you already know, like, and trust – and then filling the gaps with quality introductions from key clients and colleagues – you can quickly gain access to great professionals and build a powerfully profitable referral team.

Put the power of partnerships to work for your business. Scan this QR code or visit the link below for a video message about partnering with top trusted pros who serve your perfect prospects every day:

https://ravingreferrals.com/partner/

CHAPTER 13

Network Strategically

Another way to meet prospective referral partners is by attending networking events. In every city, there are dozens of monthly opportunities to meet other professionals. Typically hosted and led by local chambers of commerce or professional networking companies, these groups exist to help professionals and business owners connect and collaborate. That means everyone in attendance is there for the same reason you are – to meet new people in hopes of doing business together.

Have a Plan

Before investing any time going to a networking event, be sure you have a plan for who, where, and how.

- Who do you want to meet?
- Where do they usually meet?
- How will you meet them?

First, get crystal clear on the type of people you want to meet. Maybe you only want to meet a CEO, CFO, CTO, or other specific executives. Perhaps your perfect referral partner is a top producing Realtor, mortgage officer, financial advisor, or business owner. Just be clear with whom you want to connect so you can ask for an introduction when the time is right.

Second, find out where these people connect and congregate. Research local groups or events where your ideal referral partners meet and get together. The best way to do this is to call your top referral partners and ask what groups they belong to or recommend. If they belong to a chamber of commerce or networking group, you'll find them eager to invite you as their guest. These organizations typically track how many guests each member introduces to the group, so inviting guests is encouraged and celebrated.

Third, have a plan for how you will meet your ideal connections. There may only be one or two great contacts for you in the room. Rather than walking around randomly introducing yourself to strangers, ask the people running the event to introduce you to the people you want to meet. Since the event leaders check everyone in as they arrive, they meet each and every person who walks through the door. That means they are perfectly positioned to help you. You just need to ask for your ideal introduction, which is super easy when you use the following script.

Once you've checked in to the event, simply smile and say,

> "I'm wondering if you can help me. The primary reason I'm here is to find a top (CPA) that I can refer clients to and build a referral partnership with. Can you tell me if there are any quality (CPA)'s here I can connect with?"

The beauty of this question is that you are actually helping them be successful in their job. After all, the reason they are at the event is to help members and attendees connect, collaborate, and cross-refer each other. By asking for an introduction to the precise professionals you are looking to connect with, you make it easy for them to help you.

Top 10 Tips for Networking Strategically

After attending and leading networking events from coast to coast, I've learned there are ten top tips for networking success:

1. **Visualize Success** – Success starts long before you walk into any meeting or event. Remember, just one referral partner can double your business in a year or even less. As you think about the event, visualize exactly who you want to meet. Get clear on the industry they are in and have a plan for how you would like to work together. Then, before the event, take a few moments and envision yourself having a great time meeting an incredible referral partner in that industry who has been looking for someone just like you to help their clients. As you visualize the future you want to create, you activate the law of attraction, which is always good to have working for you.
2. **Bring A Buddy** – Invite one of your referral partners to join you and work the room together. Before the event, get clear on who each person is looking to meet. Then, as you meet a potential match for your referral partner, make an enthusiastic introduction to the person you just met. This helps you add value to both parties and elevate your status in their eyes. Be sure to praise and edify your networking buddy to help them feel good and raise their perceived status. As you help your referral partners succeed, they will naturally return the favor and go out of their way to help you in return. WIN–WIN–WIN.
3. **Meet The Leaders** – Introduce yourself to the people hosting the event. They are often servant leaders dedicated to helping people succeed. Since they have the respect of the

members, when they make an introduction, people take the meeting. Befriend these folks, and you will win faster.

4. **Ask For Introductions** – Ask the event leaders for introductions to the top pros they know in your target profession. Simply say,

   "The main reason I am here is that I'm looking for a quality (CPA) to whom I can refer my clients. Do you happen to know any good (CPA)s you would recommend I connect with?"

   If they know trustworthy people in that industry, they will be happy to help and make an introduction.

5. **Be Confident** – First impressions matter. As you meet new people, smile, look them in the eye, and introduce yourself confidently with a firm handshake. When you exude confidence, people feel it. Especially if they have a high nurturing personality style. The truth is that while you are interviewing potential partners, they are evaluating you as well. Show them you are comfortable in your own skin and confident in your ability to get the job done right. Your confidence will give them confidence in you.

6. **Ask Quality Questions** – Show you are interested by asking great questions to learn about the people you're meeting. If you aren't a natural networker, just ask:

   Who? What? When? Where? Why?

   - Who is your ideal client?
   - What is the primary problem you solve?
   - When do people most need your services?

- Where do you get most of your clients currently?
- Why did you choose this industry?

The answers to these questions will give you quick clarity as to how well you trust this person and how well they match your perfect partner profile.

7. **Listen And Learn** – You're here to meet good people to partner with, not to sell. After asking each question, really listen to what the person is telling you. Study what they say both verbally and non-verbally. You'll learn a lot about them in a very short time. As you listen, ask yourself if you like this person and can see yourself eventually feeling comfortable referring your clients to them.

8. **Schedule A Discovery Call** – Your primary goal for attending any networking event should be to schedule one-on-one discovery calls with *Perfect Prospects* or referral partners. Rather than trying to have a meaningful conversation in a busy, crowded, noisy environment, ask to schedule a one-on-one call at a later date. When you find someone who may be a fit, simply say,

From what you've shared, I have a number of clients who might benefit from what you do. Can we get together another time so I can ask you a few questions? Maybe next Tuesday afternoon or Wednesday morning?

What works best for you?

9. **Be Brief, Be Brilliant, Be Gone** Once you have synced calendars and scheduled a discovery call, thank them for their time and excuse yourself from the conversation. Don't overstay your welcome. Always leave them wanting more.

10. **Follow-Up and Follow-Through** – As you know, the fortune is in the follow-up. After the event, think about each person you met and send an email, text, or direct message to those with whom you want to explore relationships. If you scheduled a discovery call, send a calendar invite with the date, time, and location or description of how you will connect. You may also want to send a friend or connection request on social media to accelerate the trust-building process.

When you follow these top ten networking tips, you will build your referral team quickly and easily.

Networking Groups

In addition to referral mixers and events, you may also want to join a chamber of commerce, MeetUp, or a structured referral group like LeTip and BNI. While chambers allow unlimited members per industry, referral groups often only allow one member per profession, which is great if they have an opening in your industry.

When I was starting out in the mortgage business, I joined a chapter of LeTip International in Beaverton, Oregon. The fifteen members of this chapter met for breakfast every Thursday at 7:00 am sharp. Breaking bread together each week was a great way to get to know each other and build long-term relationships and referral partnerships. It was awesome to have a team of people committed to helping each other win and constantly scouting for opportunities for each other.

In 2013, I was referred to LeTip CEO Kim Marie Branch-Pettid, a wonderful woman committed to helping businesses grow faster together. Having visited her international headquarters many times and spent time with her, her husband, and her executive teams over the years, I can tell you her organization goes above and beyond to help their members grow their businesses, with chapters nationwide from coast-to-coast. Each chapter hosts a weekly online or in-person meeting, along with evening mixer events and large-scale conferences.

The entire LeTip referral machine has been built to ensure every member receives massive value. Each chapter has officers who lead the meetings following a regimented agenda set by LeTip headquarters. Guests are welcomed warmly and thrilled to find so many opportunities to build relationships with quality professionals.

After announcements are made, each attendee is asked to quickly stand and share their message of who and how they help. Then they report new referrals and business opportunities they have given or received from members of the group.

Referrals are tracked on their proprietary Wired platform which helps each club track and measure the business passed and the return on investment (ROI) each member has received from the group. Those who refer most are celebrated and sought after. To search for a LeTip chapter in your area, visit LeTip.com.

Dr. Ivan Misner took the LeTip concept and created his own organization called Business Networking International (BNI) back in January of 1985. Over the decades, this organization has grown to be a global powerhouse with over 270,000 members worldwide.

Although I've never been an official BNI member, I've attended countless chapter meetings and conferences over the decades. I've also had the great honor and pleasure of meeting BNI founder Dr. Ivan Misner, who is largely considered the godfather of networking. He is a humble servant eager to educate and empower as many people as possible. That's just one of the reasons BNI members are so passionate and loyal to the BNI company and community. With over 9,500 chapters, you can find a group near you at BNI.com.

The largest event-based networking organization in the U.S. is Network After Work. Rather than weekly alliance meetings, they host monthly mixer events in every major market in the U.S. Network After Work has hosted over 4,000 events over the past decade attracting over 600,000 attendees. Over that time, they have created over fifteen million business connections, which is an astonishing accomplishment.

Every Network After Work event I've attended has had over 100 guests and had plenty of prominent people to connect with. One of their brilliant networking innovations is using color coded name badges to instantly convey the industry you are in. That helps you work quickly to identify people in the industries in which you are looking to connect.

Network After Work now offers virtual events and online education as well to complement the in-person events they produce. What impresses me most about their events is that they attract the highest quality people I've met at any networking event I've ever been to.

While most networking groups tend to attract small business owners and professionals, Network After Work events also attract executives and decision makers from major corporations. This is much more of a white-collar crowd, so it's an excellent gathering place if you're looking to meet B2B clients or referral partners. Check out their schedule of events at NetworkAfterWork.com.

We've compiled a list of great networking organizations and referral groups at the end of this book. There's no substitute for meeting people in the real world, so go find a local group and start networking strategically.

THE FORTUNE IS IN THE FOLLOW-UP

As you start networking, you will be meeting some awesome people that can send you a lot of business. Your goal should be to get into the know, like, trust zone as quickly as possible.

Connect with them on social media and be sure to like, comment, share, retweet, and invite them often and you can accelerate the trust building process.

A tactic I learned from Casey Eberhart in his awesome Networking Riches course is his ATM social strategy:

1. ADD people to your FB group
2. TAG them in the post
3. MESSAGE them personally

Do this consistently and you'll start attracting great referral partners who send you a steady stream of *Perfect Prospects.* Before you attend another networking event, be sure to scan this QR code or visit the link below to learn the top three networking quick tips. Share with your professional network to add value and help them accelerate their success:

Ravingreferrals.com/network

CHAPTER 14

Create Your Referral Alliance

After 43 years of living in the rain forest of Oregon, my wife and I decided to move our family down to the sunny blue skies of Phoenix, Arizona in 2014. That meant leaving behind the hundreds of professionals with whom I had spent decades creating relationships and building an entirely new tribe down in the desert.

Connect With Connectors

I started my Phoenix networking tour at a Network After Work event because they always draw a great crowd. When I arrived, I met Danielle, the leader of the event who I quickly connected with, shared who I was looking to meet, and asked for introductions to top trusted pros. This led to some great conversations, for which I thanked Danielle at the end of the night.

The next day, I connected with her and started building a long-term relationship over the months that followed. From that connection came a referral to James Miller, the CEO of Network After Work who I've since built a relationship and profitable partnership with. Remember, the leaders of these events know everyone and are happy to make introductions.

Next, I found NetworkingPhoenix.com which combined all the daily networking events throughout the Valley into one centralized site and calendar. With over 40,000 members with searchable profiles on their platform, this group helps you stay connected long after you've met. Brilliant!

While the website helped me locate the various events taking place locally, I was really drawn to meet the leader behind it all – a woman named Gelie Ahkenblit. I attended one of her signature events and followed these same steps I've just shared with you. Meet the leader, ask for introductions to the people you want to meet, report back to the leader thanking them for the introductions. Rinse and repeat.

Over the following months of building a relationship with Gelie, I learned she is passionate about speaking and coaching, so when producing my Profit Partners Summit, I was thrilled when Gelie agreed to share her wisdom with our audience. This gave me an opportunity to give back and support her in fulfilling her mission.

Over the months that followed, I attended the Phoenix Metro Chamber of Commerce, led by Jason Bressler, Network Together led by Robert and Shawn Jones, and Networking360 led by Thomas and Melina Evans. Each of these people are amazing local leaders committed to helping businesspeople connect and collaborate. They go above and beyond to help people succeed and will do everything they can to connect you to people that bring value to your life.

It was fascinating seeing the differences in the type of people each group attracted. Each organization had their own culture, which varied based on the leader. Some emphasized education and impact, while others focused on cocktails and connections.

As you explore your local networking options, look for leaders you admire and respect. When you attend, introduce yourself to the leaders, ask for introductions, and report your results back to the leader thanking them for the connection. Then, make it your mission to build relationships with these influencers. You will find they will eagerly connect you with your perfect prospects and potential referral partners.

The reason I'm sharing these stories with you is to illustrate what is possible when you apply the *Raving Referrals* system. Create a vision and plan for using these events to connect with your *Perfect Prospects* and referral partners, and both your network and net worth will grow. Be strategic and you can meet powerful people and build profitable partnerships quickly and consistently.

Invite Your Trusted Team

If you are serious about taking your business to new heights, consider starting your own personal referral group or what we call a *Referral Alliance.* For best results, bring together your best referral partners and ask them to join you in launching your own group. As you unite your team, you elevate your status and establish yourself as a leader and influential connector.

The best way to accomplish this quickly and easily is to schedule a meeting at your office, a restaurant, or even via zoom. Simply choose a time and location then send a quick message to each person inviting them to attend.

Say something like:

> "Hi (name), as you may know, I am in the process of expanding my business, and I'm creating an alliance of vetted and trusted professionals I can refer my clients to. I truly value our relationship and would like to invite you to be a core member of my referral team. I will be gathering my most important referral partners (date/time) at (location) and hope you can attend.
>
> Please let me know if you can join us."

For best results, send a calendar invite to each person you want to attend so they have the date, time, and location already in their calendar. That makes it super easy for them to accept your invite with one quick click. This also helps you see who is interested, available, and committed to attending. You may also want to create an event on Facebook, LinkedIn or another social network if you are connected to these people on those platforms.

Your Alliance Meeting

As your group gathers, you may have a few early arrivals. Welcome them warmly and let them know when your meeting will begin. If you are not an extrovert or natural nurturer, you may want to have an assistant greet your guests, so they feel the love from the get-go.

Start your meeting by greeting the group and thanking them for attending. Ask each person to introduce themselves and describe who they help and how they help. Once everyone has introduced themselves, simply review some of the co-marketing campaigns outlined in the *Referral Partner Blueprint* outlined in Chapter 16.

Here's a script you can use as a guideline:

Greeting

"Thank you for coming today. The reason I asked you all to join me is that I am expanding my business and creating an alliance of vetted and trusted professionals I'll be referring my clients to.

I truly value each and every one of you and view you as one of the best in your respective industries. Not only am I hoping to do more business with you personally, but I also want to connect each of you so you can do more business together.

After all, everyone in this room serves (consumers/homeowners/business owners) so we share the same ideal client and can grow our businesses faster and further by cross-referring and cross-promoting each other."

Introductions

What I'd like to do now is go around the room and give everyone a chance to introduce themselves and share who you help and how you help. That will help everyone here understand the services you provide and who your perfect prospects and ideal clients are.

Before you leave, I'd like to ask you each to fill out a *Referral Partner Optimization Form* so I can train my team on what type of clients we should refer to you.

I'll go first. As you all know, my name is ______________ and I help ____________________ *(share your Service Statement).*

To give you an example of what I do, I recently had a client who _____________. *(share a story of a problem you solved and the difference it made for them).*

> I'm passionate about helping people ____________ and a great referral for me is a (share your *Perfect Prospect Profile*). Before we move on, does anyone have any questions about the services I provide?

Answer any questions that come up and remember to tell success stories so people can visualize who and how you help. Telling a memorable story of someone you've helped turns people into referral scouts because when they hear someone facing the challenge you solve, they will immediately think of you.

> *"Hopefully, that gives you more clarity on how I can help your clients and customers. Now let's go around the room starting to my left."*

After each person shares who and how they help, be sure to compliment and edify them to boost their confidence and status among your guests. Your job is to help everyone feel honored and special.

Share stories of how these people have helped you or your clients in the past. Describe what you appreciate most about each person, and you will instantly expand your value in their eyes. This process ensures people view you as the connector and influencer you are. It also locks in their loyalty and commitment to doing business with you going forward.

Instructions

Once all attendees have shared who and how they help, share your plan for doing more business together. Using the *Referral Partner Blueprint* in Chapter 16 as a guide, mention some of the strategies you plan to use to introduce your trusted referral partners to your clients and colleagues. This will give them a vision for how they will win more business through your *Referral Alliance.*

We recommend your strategy include interviews with your referral partners to add value to them and build their credibility in the eyes of your clients. Simply record a quick zoom interview and post the video recording on Facebook, YouTube, and/or LinkedIn. Alternatively, you can broadcast your conversation live on these platforms as well.

Wrap-Up

As you conclude your Alliance meeting, thank each person for attending and let them know you'd like to schedule a one-to-one conversation with them to plan out how you can grow your businesses together. Be sure each person leaves with your *Referral Kit,* business cards, referral cards, brochures, and any other marketing materials you'd like them to give to their clients when they recommend your services. That way, each Referral Partner leaves empowered to refer you quickly and consistently.

Hang-Out

If your schedule allows, recommend they hang out and connect with the people in the room who would be the best fit for their business. You will add additional value by connecting them with other business owners and professionals with whom they can build relationships. Plus, the more time you spend with each person, the more likely they are to send profitable prospects your way.

Consider printing a form each Partner fills out so you have a written record of who they help, how they help, how they want to be referred, and a success story you can share with your clients.

Raving Referrals Partner Profile

Name: ______________________________

Company: ______________________________

Profession: ______________________________

Phone: ______________________________

Who are your Perfect Prospects?

How would you describe your perfect prospects and ideal clients?

____

____

____

____

____

How do you help?

What is most important for me to share about your product or service? What makes you unique?

____

____

____

____

____

How would you like me to refer you?

Do you offer free consultations or any special promotions you'd like me to share?

____

____

____

____

____

What's your best success story?

Share your best client result or testimonial so I can retell the story to my clients.

____

____

____

____

____

Following these steps will help you create a highly productive and profi table referral alliance you can build your business with for years to come. The best part is that a client for one of you can be a client for all of you. Once you attract a new client for your business, think about which of your referral partners you can introduce them to. There are likely other services this client would benefi t from. As you refer them to your partners, and they refer their clients to you, everyone wins together.

Building a strong Referral Alliance can help you attract *Raving* Referrals for years to come. Scan this QR code or visit the link below for a video message about creating powerful and profitable partnering with companies and professionals who are committed to your success:

https://ravingreferrals.com/alliance

CHAPTER 15

Leverage LinkedIn

Another way to enroll referral partners is to activate your LinkedIn connections converting these people from causal connections to active referrers for your business.

Everyone knows LinkedIn can be a powerful source of new business. However, most people have a ton of LinkedIn connections that just sit there idle, doing nothing for their business. The good news is that you can mine the acres of diamonds you are sitting on by activating your LinkedIn connections, so they introduce you to your perfect partners and prospects.

This strategy requires some research and preparation, but the results are definitely worth the effort. Especially if you serve business owners or provide services to businesses.

The *LinkedIn Activation* strategy consists of six steps:

1. **Research** your contact's LinkedIn connections and identify five people to ask them about.
2. **Invite** your contact to talk on the phone or over lunch about their LinkedIn connections.
3. **Ask** about their connections with a goal of getting two to three introductions or referrals.

4. **Thank** your contact for the introductions and referrals.
5. **Reach Out** to each referred person.
6. **Follow-Up** with your contact and let them know how things went.

Step 1: Research

Once you have identified the desired professions for your Power Team of referral partners, LinkedIn is a great way to research the connections of people who already know, like, and trust you so you can effectively ask for introductions to those you want to meet.

Even if you've done a great job connecting with your contacts on a personal level and they want to refer people to you, it can be difficult for them to effectively think through all of their contacts to identify who they should refer to you. To make the process easier for them, take a few minutes to research the LinkedIn connections of your strongest relationships and identify the people you'd like to get introduced to. After all, no one knows your perfect prospects and ideal referral partners better than you.

Strive to pick just five LinkedIn connections to ask about. Ultimately, your goal should be to receive two or three referrals and introductions from each of your contacts. If you ask about more than five people, it can feel a bit burdensome and overwhelming for them.

When you choose less than five, you decrease your chance of receiving referrals/introductions since they may not have very deep relationships with each of the people you've chosen and will not be able to make many introductions for you. Plus, you can always circle back to them and ask for additional introductions once you've connected with their initial contacts.

In order to begin the process, you must be connected with your contacts on LinkedIn, and they must allow their connections to be able to search their contacts (which most people do). So, if you are not connected with them, send them a connection request.

Search Strategically

Searching your contacts connections can seem overwhelming and extremely time consuming. Many of your contacts may have 500 or more connections. Fortunately, there is a very effective and time-saving approach you can use to filter your contacts' connections and view only their most relevant connections.

Step A: Log in to your LinkedIn account.

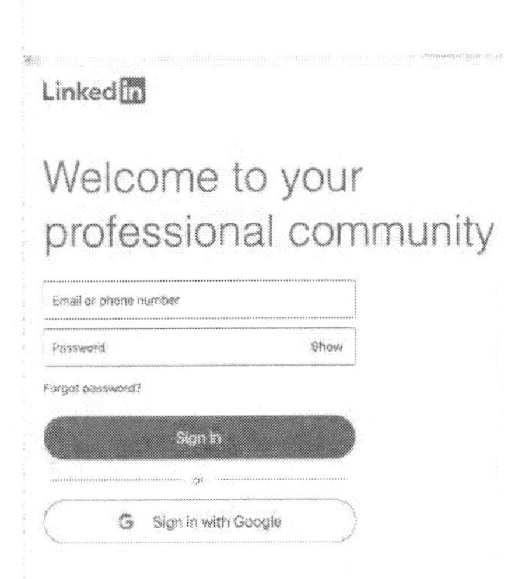

Step B: Enter the name of the contact you want to ask for referrals. Click the search button.

One of my favorite people on the planet is Gail Watson, President, and founder of WSA, the Women Speakers Association. Gail empowers women everywhere to share their voice as a paid public speaker. Over the past decade, WSA has helped tens of thousands of women get seen, booked, and paid all over the world. Gail has an amazing global network of influencers, so if I were looking for an introduction, I would locate her LinkedIn profile and click the Connections link under her name, title, and location.

What you will see is a list of your contact's connections sorted by what LinkedIn believes is most relevant for you.

Step C: Enter a job title for your ideal prospects and/or connectors. For example, if you are a business coach, you might want to search the following job titles:

- CEO
- Business Owner
- President
- Entrepreneur
- Estate Planning Attorney
- Business Attorney
- Insurance Agent
- Financial Advisor
- Banker
- Mortgage Broker

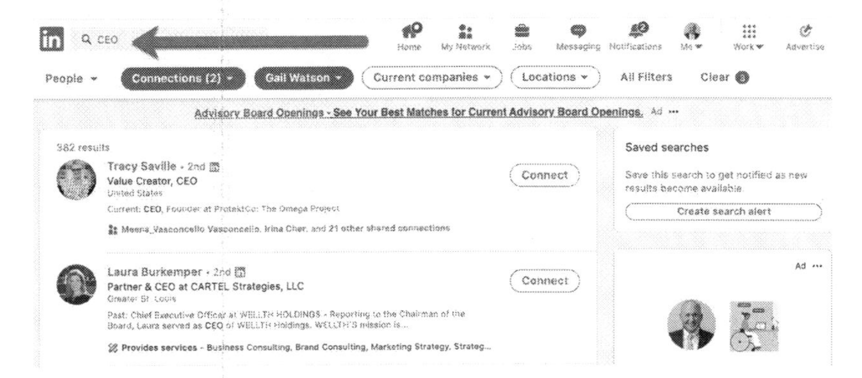

Step D: Click on "Locations" and enter your city if you want to narrow the results.

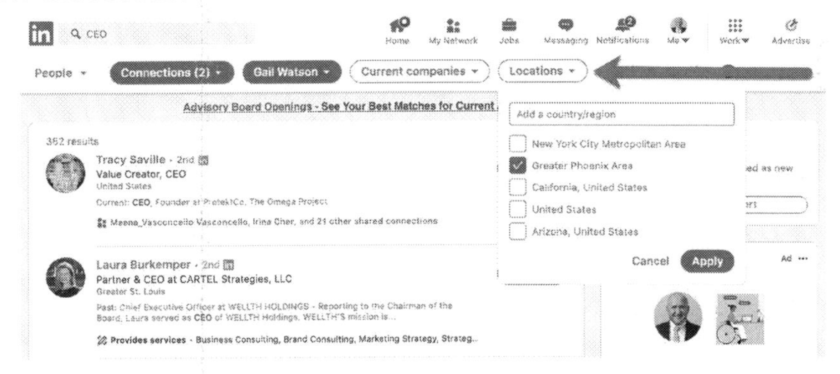

Step E: This will give you a targeted list of their contacts that most closely match the type of professionals you are looking to connect with. Just review the search results and pick up to five people to ask your contact about.

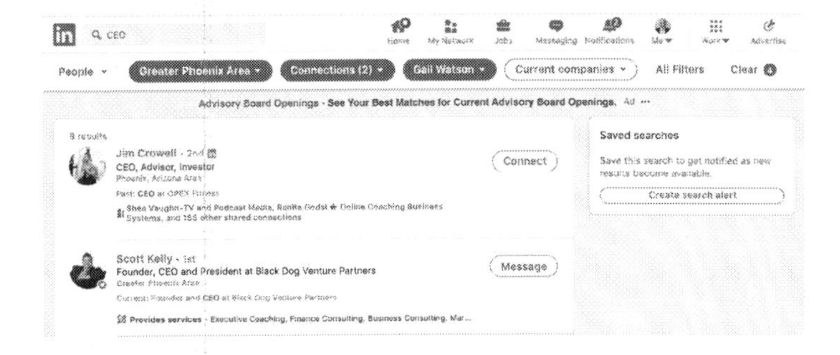

If more results are needed, simply repeat these steps using a different job title. Once you have found five people to ask your contact about, it is time to send your contact an invitation.

Step 2: Invite

Once you've identified people you'd like to be introduced to, it's time to reach out to your contact and invite them to connect so you can ask them about these five LinkedIn connections.

Sample Email Invitation:

> Hi Gail,
>
> Hope all is well in your world. I'm reaching out because I am looking to expand my network of business contacts and noticed you are connected to a few people on LinkedIn that I'd like to meet. I have a few contacts I think you would benefit from meeting as well.
>
> Do you have a few minutes to jump on a quick call so we can connect and collaborate? Let me know what day and time works best for your schedule.
>
> All My Best, Brandon

Messaging them before you call allows them to prepare for the conversation, so you don't catch them off guard. Identify a few people you can introduce your contact to. Then start by giving them an introduction to add value to them and their business.

Step 3: Ask

Prior to your call or meeting, print off the profiles of the five LinkedIn connections with whom you would like to be introduced. That will make it easy for you to share what interests you in that person.

During your conversation, remind your contact that you were viewing their LinkedIn profile and had a few questions about some of their connections. Then simply share the list of profiles you've printed.

Ask questions you have about each person, such as:

- How well do you know them?
- Have you done much business with them in the past?
- What can you tell me about them and their company?
- What types of clients do they serve?
- Do you recommend this person to others?
- Do you think this would be a good person for me to connect with?

After hearing about each person, if you decide you would like to meet this person, simply ask to be introduced by saying something like:

> "Stephen really sounds like an interesting person I would love to meet. Would you mind introducing the two of us? Or, if you would prefer, I am happy to send an email and mention you had great things to say about him and I would like to get to know him myself."

This is an important statement because you are giving your contact the choice of how the introduction will take place. If your contact knows the person really well and consistently communicates with them, they will likely feel comfortable making the introduction personally.

However, if your contact is busy or hasn't had any recent contact with that person, they might prefer that you reach out, introduce yourself directly, and use their name and recommendation as a reason for connecting.

The goal is to get at least two to three introductions from each of your contacts. If you get two or three introductions before asking about all five of their LinkedIn connections, stop asking so you don't overwhelm them. You can always ask about others later.

Step 4: Give Thanks

After your calls, be sure to follow up with your contacts to: (1) thank them for their time and introductions, (2) remind them of who each agreed to introduce you to, and (3) let them know you will be following up to let them know how things turned out.

Sample Thank You Email:

"It was great connecting with you today. Thanks for helping me learn about some of your LinkedIn Connections. I really appreciate your willingness to introduce me to these people.

To make it easy for you, I've written the introduction below so you can just copy and paste into an email or direct message to [referral #1] and [referral #2].

Thanks again. This really means a lot to me. I'll let you know how things turn out."

[Insert e-introduction here]

Step 5: Outreach

If you agreed to introduce yourself directly, be sure you start your call, message, or email by sharing the name of the person who referred you and why they thought the two of you should connect.

Sample LinkedIn Connection Request:

SUBJECT: Gail Watson suggested we connect

> "Hi Nancy, I met with Gail Watson the other day and she had great things to say about you and suggested we connect. I would love to get to know you and find out more about your business. Would you like to chat and collaborate?"

If your contact made the introduction on your behalf, follow up with the referred person as soon as possible after the introduction. This way, you are already on their radar and will be more likely to take your call and agree to a meeting.

Sample Outreach Email:

SUBJECT: Gail Watson suggested we connect

> Hello <name>, I was talking with Gail Watson, and she suggested you and I connect. Gail had some great things to say about you, so I'd love to connect on a quick call or zoom. Sounds like we may have some great business possibilities together.
>
> What does your schedule look like next week? Do you have a few minutes to talk on the phone?
>
> Let me know what works best for you. You can reply to this email or give me a call back at (xxx) xxx-xxx

Step 6: Follow Up

After you've connected with the people your contact has introduced, be sure to let the person who made the introductions know what happened with each referral. Just send a quick email or direct message with a quick summary of each conversation you had.

Sample Follow-up Email:

"Hi Gail. Thanks again for the introductions you made last week. You know some great people, and I wanted to send you a quick update on our conversations:

Shelly Anderson – We had lunch together and have already started working together. Shelly is everything you said she was. Thanks again for the great referral.

James Smith – Briefly spoke and we're meeting next week.

Andrew Lewis – I sent an email but haven't heard back yet."

If you strike gold with one of their contacts and they end up becoming a client or referral partner, thank them immediately so they can celebrate your success. You may even want to send them a thank you card or gift card so they feel appreciated. Recognizing and thanking people for making referrals and introductions is an important step in the *Raving Referrals* system.

This *LinkedIn Activation* strategy can help you grow your network quickly. Just two introductions from ten people will bring you twenty new potential clients and/or referral partners. That's one new conversation for each business day of the month.

Make Your Meetings Matter

Before meeting with someone you've never met, spend a few minutes researching them online. Check out their website, LinkedIn profile, and social media accounts to see what common interests you have. Nothing builds rapport faster than sharing your love for the same university, charity or football team.

When you're meeting with your prospective partner, you always want to give value first before asking for anything from them. Focus on helping them achieve their goals. The faster and more effectively you do that, the faster they will feel like they know, like, and trust you enough to refer their valuable clients to you.

When you first connect, consider starting the conversation by saying,

> "Thanks for meeting with me today. I've heard a lot of great things about you. You come highly recommended. The reason I wanted to meet with you is that I serve a lot of (type of client – homeowners/business owners) who may be able to use your services. I'm hoping to learn more about you and your business so I'm referring you the right type of clients."

5 Power Questions for Prospective Partners

Now your job is to ask questions and listen closely to learn all you can about this person. These five questions will get your conversations going:

1. How long have you been in this line of work? This is an easy, disarming question that is natural and comfortable to ask. What you are really looking to understand and evaluate is how much expertise they have in their field. Ask yourself if this is someone to which you would feel comfortable and confident entrusting your clients to. Once they have given an overview of their experience and expertise, you can ask the second power question, which is:

2. What do you like best about what you do?
   This question is designed to uncover their WHY. What is their passion and purpose behind their profession? You are looking for their motivation beyond just the money. Ideally, they will share a client success story you can

later retell to some of your clients when referring them to this person. Mostly though, you are trying to discern and decide if this person shares the same values that you do and would be someone you would trust to serve your clients. Once they have shared their WHY, simply ask power question #3:

3. How would you describe your ideal client?

   This question will help you understand if you truly share the same *Perfect Prospect Profile*. If it sounds like they are describing your ideal clients, you know this is a great fit for a prospective partner. If not, you can still be good referral sources for each other from time to time. Either way, you should follow up by asking the 4th power question which is:

4. What would you say is your biggest business challenge?

   The reason you want to ask this question is that for most professionals, the answer to this question is that they want more prospects, more clients, and more business. If they respond saying they need more clients, you've uncovered a great opportunity to steer the conversation towards creating a strategic alliance and building your businesses together. First though, you should gain more information about their current business development efforts by asking the final power question:

5. Where do most of your clients come from?

   Usually, the answer to this question will be referrals, at which point you can say something like:

   "I'm glad to hear referrals are important to you. I work almost exclusively by referral which is exactly why I am here today.

> As I mentioned earlier, I'm looking for quality people I can partner with to grow our businesses together. Based on what you shared about your business, you are definitely the type of person I'm looking to add to my trusted team of professionals to which I promote and refer my clients.
>
> Just to give you a little more background on me...."

Now share some information about yourself and the services you provide that are most in alignment with what they shared their clients need. Then, share your *Perfect Prospect Profile* and *Service Statement* so they are clear on who you are looking to serve and how you help those clients solve their challenges and live better lives.

LinkedIn is a goldmine for creating new business opportunities. Especially if you are in B2B sales where businesses and business professionals are your perfect prospects.

Scan this QR code or visit the link below for a video message on how to leverage LinkedIn and get people you know to introduce you to their best clients and LinkedIn connections. Then, share this video on LinkedIn and watch the comments and likes roll in.

https://ravingreferrals.com/linkedin/

Now it's time for you to build a strong referral partnership which is easy using the *Referral Partner Blueprint* we will cover in the next chapter.

CHAPTER 16

The Referral Partner Blueprint

The fastest and easiest way to build referral partnerships is by using the *Referral Partner Blueprint*. This easy-to-use system gives you a paint-by-numbers approach to guide people through a collaboration conversation.

Once you've identified someone you would like to form a referral partnership with, simply pull out the *Referral Partner Blueprint* to guide your conversation.

Discuss the cross-promotion strategies you think will work best for this particular referral partnership. Check off what each person is willing to do for the other so both parties have a clear agreement in place.

As you follow the format and fill in the blanks, you will find it makes the process of creating referral partnerships with complementary professionals, virtually dummy proof.

Referral Partner Blueprint

To create a mutually prosperous relationship, both parties agree to

- Introduce each other to prospective referral partners
- Recommend each other to clients & colleagues
- Invite each other to participate in joint client consultations if appropriate
- Cross-Promote each other through:

01. Introductions
02. Client Referrals
03. Rating and Reviews
04. Special Offers
05. Gift Certificates
06. Consultations
07. Referral Cards
08. Websites
09. Social Posts
10. Newsletters
11. Team Brochures
12. Bundled Offers
13. Direct Mail
14. Client Events
15. Sponsorships
16. Workshops
17. Podcasts
18. Video Interviews
19. Webinars
20. Referral Mixers
21. Charity Champions Campaigns

We will cover each of these cross-promotion campaigns in the next chapter. First, you need to understand how to educate and empower your referral partners to send you new client opportunities quickly and consistently.

Train Your Team

As you start using the *Referral Partner Blueprint*, you will find people are eager to partner with you. That's why it's important to train your referral partners on the specific clients you are looking for, and how best to refer you.

To ensure you attract a steady stream of profitable prospects coming to your business, follow these five proven steps:

1. Discuss your *Perfect Prospect Profile* and *Service Statement* so they understand how you help and what challenges you solve.
2. Share stories of clients you've helped so they will remember and refer you when a client mentions facing a similar challenge.
3. Supply them with your *Referral Kit* including brochures and business cards they can set out in their lobby and give to their clients.
4. Create customized gift certificates or referral cards so your referral partner feels special, and their clients know you are a trusted professional.
5. Print a list of your top ten Frequently Asked Questions (FAQs) so your referral partners are informed and can educate their clients about the services you provide.

These are the top five ways you can empower your partners. The key is to help them understand how you help so you become their go-to, number one trusted resource for each and every client who faces the problems you solve. The more you educate your referral partners on the value you provide, the more clients they will send your way. So long as you follow up consistently.

Follow-Up and Follow Through

After you've met with each prospective referral partner, be sure to follow up and follow through on any commitments you made. Take action immediately, and you will impress them with your professionalism. If you committed to making introductions, make them quickly and effectively. Go above and beyond to gain your new referral partners respect and reciprocity.

Be sure to update and thank the person who made the introduction. Give them an overview of how well the conversation went and whether you believe this person will be a fit for your clients. Following up honors the introducer and shows them you take good care of the introductions they give you. Often, this alone leads to more referrals because you are demonstrating your professionalism in communication.

If you're really serious about building a solid referral base, you may want to send whoever introduced you a thank you card or small gift as a token of appreciation. This will lead them one step closer to singing your praises to everyone they know. The more people feel you care, the more they will care about you.

Play the Long Game

One thing you need to understand is that building referral partnerships takes time. Although you will likely receive referrals from some partners quickly, others will need to know, like and trust you over time. The more relational equity you build with people, the more referrals you will receive.

Rather than expecting instant results, make a goal for how many referral partnerships you plan to create over the coming year. Keeping your eye on the prize will help you build a solid business that will generate profitable prospects for years to come.

Connect with the people you want to do business with regularly. Calendar consistent communications to them every two weeks at a minimum. Seeing them in person always creates the deepest connections but isn't the most time efficient. That's why you want to mix in regular phone calls, text messages, video messages, emails, and social media messages to stay top-of-mind and continually add value.

Before reaching out, think of a way you can add value to them and their clients. Never call saying you are just "checking in". That is one of the worst statements you can make because you are telling them you have no other reason to call other than to ask them for business. Instead, you could:

- Give them a referral
- Provide an update on a client they referred.
- Offer to connect them with a professional or business owner.
- Share an idea you think will help their business.
- Ask a question about their industry or the services they provide.
- Offer to promote them using one of the co-marketing campaigns in the next chapter.
- Invite them to join you at an industry or networking event.
- Let them know about new products or services you are adding.
- Share industry insights you think they should know about.
- Stop by to drop off gifts, books, brochures, or branded swag.

It's A Numbers Game

Using these strategies and scripts can make a profound impact on your business over the months and years to come. Just imagine what your business will look like 12 months from now if you take the time to meet just one new prospective partner each week for the next year.

Of those 50 people, if only 20% are a fit and become your referral partners, you will have 10 new professionals referring you profitable clients consistently for years to come. Then, for the rest of your career, you will be on easy street never having to wonder where your next client is coming from. In reality, most professionals experience much better results than partnering 20% of the time, so you can truly accelerate the process and your revenue by following the *Referral Partner Blueprint*.

Give More

When building referral partnerships, you should always be on the lookout for ways to add value to your partners. Truth is that the more you give in life, the more will be given to you. I'm such a passionate proponent of this strategy that I had customized license plates for my BMW back in Oregon that said, GIV MOR.

For me, it's much more than just a slogan. It's a life philosophy. I'm always looking to add value to everyone I meet and to give as much as humanly possible. When you adopt the GIVE MORE attitude and look for ways to practice random acts of kindness, you'll find life becomes easier in ways you would never have imagined. This might sound a little woo-woo to you right now, but in my experience, karma and the law of attraction are very real. The more you give, the more serendipity shows up in your life.

Back in 1998, my wife and I took a two-week trip to Italy and Greece. While it was tough to leave my mortgage business for two weeks,

I made sure to bring back some exotic gifts for the Realtors with whom I was building referral partnerships. In addition to some of the standard tourist trinkets, I also brought back metal bottles filled with Greek Ouzo, as well as the most delicious baklava I have ever tasted.

When I returned home and dropped off these sweet treats and exotic liqueurs to my top referral partners, they were blown away that I was thoughtful enough to think of them while on my European vacation. Especially since I had transported these gifts over 6,000 miles to bring them back something special.

Next, I travelled to Hawaii and brought back cases of chocolate covered macadamia nuts. While my referral partners enjoyed the gift, what they really appreciated is that they were important enough to me that I was thinking of them while away with my family.

The truth is that those tasty treats helped solidify relationships and win referrals worth thousands of times the cost of the gifts. While I'm sure they enjoyed what I gave them, what won them over was my generosity and thoughtfulness.

As you start building your referral partnerships, be on the lookout for ways you can make a difference in their lives. Do everything you can to give more to your partners, and you will activate the law of reciprocity and watch your business grow.

Especially when you start cross-promoting with your partners, which is the final key to profitable partnerships.

Ready to create more profitable partnerships?

The Referral Partner Blueprint makes it easy to guide your conversations and create a powerful plan where you and your referral partners get into action and win together.

Scan this QR code or visit the link below for a video message on how to use the Referral Partner Blueprint to maximize your success:

https://ravingreferrals.com/blueprint

CHAPTER 17

Top 21 Cross Promotion Campaigns

Marketing is the lifeblood of your business. Marketing is what spreads the message that brings in profitable prospects that become lifetime clients. That's why partnering and cross promoting with others who already serve your market can be the fastest and most powerful way to grow your business.

When it comes to promoting yourself and your services, there's nothing like the credibility and visibility you gain when someone else raves about you. People don't care what you say about yourself near as much as they care what others say about you.

Your goal is to get seen, get found, and get paid.

When people see your name or brand being recommended by someone they respect, they automatically trust you more and are more likely to hire you. Especially when people endorse you authentically and passionately.

Whether your goal is to attract a few ideal clients, or gain millions of fans and followers, cross promoting with influencers, experts, businesses, and professionals who serve your ideal clients can produce real results rapidly.

You've Seen This Before

Often called co-op marketing or simply co-marketing, this is a strategic marketing and advertising partnership between two or more companies or referral partners who promote each other to their respective audiences. Collaborating on a marketing campaign can help both parties generate twice the results with half the effort.

What's great about co-marketing is that both partners leverage their social sphere to generate more buzz, awareness, fans, followers, and profitable prospects together. These campaigns can quickly provide the extra boost that attracts more leads and revenues.

Even if you have never co-marketed yourself, you've seen the biggest brands on the planet doing it for years. One of the best examples is the shoe brand Nike partnering with Michael Jordan to create the Air Jordan brand. According to Forbes magazine, their partnership has generated over $1.3 billion to Michael Jordan since 1984. This alliance not only made Jordan richer than any contract from playing basketball, but it also simultaneously solidified Nike as the dominant leader in the shoe game. In Nike's 2019 fiscal year, the Jordan Brand generated $3.1 billion in sales accounting for 8% of total Nike revenue for the year.

Back in Portland, one of the fathers whose boys I coached in youth sports was the son of Reggie Saunders, Nike's Senior Director of Entertainment Marketing for Air Jordan. He was one cool cat. His stock really rose with the boys on our basketball team when he gave each player a free pair of the latest and greatest brand spanking new Air Jordans. Reggie told me story after story of the athletes the company was able to attract as partners because these players grew up wearing Air Jordans and always wanted to "Be like Mike."

The value Jordan brought Nike went far beyond shoe sales and solidified the brand as the king of the shoe game. As Nike would say, when it comes to co-marketing, JUST DO IT.

Here are a few co-marketing examples to get your wheels spinning:

CoverGirl Makeup & Star Wars

Another great example of creating profitable partnerships and co-marketing campaigns comes from the larger-than-life Shaquille O'Neal. After having a hall-of-fame career on the court, Shaq cashed in on his notoriety by creating strategic alliances with a number of companies and brands, including:

- 24 Hour Fitness
- Arizona Beverage Company
- Auntie Anne's Pretzels
- Boys & Girls Club of America
- Buick
- Carnival Cruise
- Comcast
- Dove
- Dunkman Shoes
- Epson Printers
- Five Guys Burgers & Fries
- Gold Bond
- IcyHot
- JC Penney
- Krispy Kreme
- Lining Shoes
- Macy's
- Monster Headphones
- Muscle Milk
- NBA 2k
- Nestle Crunch
- Papa John's Pizza
- Pepsi
- Reebok
- Sleep Apnea Mask
- Soupman
- Susta Sugar Substitute
- Taco Bell
- The General Insurance
- Zales Jewelry

While you may never collaborate with a major corporation like those listed above, the strategy is the same when promoting your personal services.

Now that you are aware of co-marketing campaigns, you are going to start seeing these campaigns over and over. The power and influence you can unlock through partnerships are unmatched. In fact, teenagers are now making millions as instant influencers on Instagram and TikTok partnering with companies as brand ambassadors to promote their energy drinks, clothing, makeup, and jewelry products.

The Ultimate Trust Transfer

Co-marketing gives you the ultimate marketing leverage because as you cross promote your referral partners, they transfer the trust they've built with their clients and prospects on to you.

By collaborating and cross promoting each other, both you and your partner:

- Increase awareness for each other's businesses and services
- Attract more prospects, fans, and followers
- Generate leads, referrals, and business opportunities
- Reduce marketing costs while increasing closing rates

Creating cross promotions and co-marketing campaigns with just ten other professionals or businesses over the next year can increase your marketing reach by 1,000% or more. The way this works is simple. Let's say your ideal clients are homeowners and that you have 1,000 people on your mailing list. If you partner with ten other professionals who also serve homeowners with similar size databases, you are now being promoted, endorsed, and recommended to 10,000 prospective clients in addition to your own 1,000 contacts.

Plus, by helping your partners gain more visibility and grow their books of business, you dramatically increase the likelihood they will return the favor by promoting and referring you to their clients and colleagues.

So how can you leverage the power of co-marketing to promote your products and services in your local market?

Glad you asked!

21 Top Cross Promotion Campaigns

As you meet with prospective Referral Partners to create a strategic alliance, just pull out your *Referral Partner Blueprint* to guide your conversation. This powerful tool will help you steer your discussions through the various ways you and your partners can cross-promote each other to win more business together.

The basic strategy for each of these campaigns is for you and your partners to promote and recommend each other to your respective databases and social spheres.

The top 21 ways you and your partners can proactively promote or recommend each other are:

1. Introductions
2. Client Referrals
3. Ratings and Reviews
4. Special Offers
5. Gift Certificates
6. Consultations
7. Referral Cards
8. Websites
9. Social Posts
10. Newsletters
11. Team Brochures
12. Bundled Offers
13. Direct Mail
14. Client Events

15. Sponsorships
16. Workshops
17. Podcasts
18. Video Interviews
19. Webinars
20. Referral Mixers
21. Charity Champion Campaigns

1 – Introductions

When meeting with a new Referral Partner, an easy YES to get things moving is making introductions to other professionals you each know. After all, your new referral partner likely knows some great prospective partners for you. Can you imagine what life will be like when people start referring you to their best clients who are a pleasure to work with. Think about the difference you will be able to make in other people's businesses. As we work together and cross-refer through our Referral Alliances, WE ALL WIN TOGETHER.

The reason to start with making introductions is that it is an easy ask you both should be very comfortable moving forward with. Starting the conversation by getting them to agree to something small will increase the likelihood they will agree on other campaigns later on.

Remember to give first. Start by suggesting a few people you know might be a good prospective partner for them. Tell them about each person and offer to introduce them. You might even want to set up a zoom or face-to-face meeting with the three of you so you can meet socially.

The beauty is that every time these people talk to each other in the future, they will inevitably talk about you. After all, you are the one thing they always have in common. Naturally, one of them will ask the other if they have talked to you lately and how you are doing. That means the more introductions you make, the more often you are coming up in other people's conversations, which keeps you and your business top of mind.

Once you've suggested a few introductions, the other person will likely offer some people they can introduce you to. This is where you want to make sure you communicate exactly what types of professionals you want to be introduced to. The clearer you are, the more likely they are to connect you with quality professionals who have the ability to refer a lot of Perfect Prospects your way.

2 – Client Referrals

Next, we suggest you discuss referring each other to your respective clients. As you start sending each other new client opportunities, both partners win more business together. Again, start by giving first and mention that you have quite a few clients you can refer their way. If you have a referral you can give them there and then, even better. The more you refer them, the more they will reciprocate.

Explain that as you build referral partnerships, you are always scouting and looking out for new clients you can introduce to your partners. If that sounds like something they are interested in, you would be happy to proactively refer them clients and hope they will do the same for you.

Then simply ask them how that sounds. Their response will tell you a lot. If they sound hesitant, they either may not be the right partner you are looking for, or they need time to get to know, like, and trust you more before committing to that level of alliance.

3 – Ratings and Reviews

Another way to help your referral partners boost their credibility and visibility is to give each other ratings or reviews on Google,

Yelp, Angi's List, HOA.com, or any other sites and services where you each promote yourselves. Just ask your partner if they use ratings and reviews in their marketing and if they'd like you to give them a rating or review. You should also let them know which sites you are using and see if they'd be willing to give you a rating or review. You can even get it done right then before you end your meeting.

The importance of reviews cannot be overstated. Recently, I was in New York City for a C-Suite Network event led by its charismatic CEO Jeffrey Hayzlett. During the conference, I was talking with the SVP of Global Strategic Partnerships and Business Development for the Amazon company Audible. Helena shared that Audible now uses reviews as their top marketing strategy to drive revenue. Their testing shows member reviews are far more effective in attracting and retaining new subscribers. In the online world, reviews rule. If a tech giant like Audible who has done extensive marketing research believes in the power of reviews, so should you.

We humans trust the collective power of reviews because we feel like the research has been done for us. Again, people care far more what other people say about you than what you say about yourself. Especially when those people are high Blueprint or Knowledge personality types.

4 – Special Offers

Everyone loves to save money and get a deal. That's why offering special discounts is another great way to help your partners promote your products or services. This helps your partners give their clients something special and gives your partners and gives them an easy way to introduce your services.

Depending on your industry, you might offer 10% or $100 off for new customers who are introduced by your partner. Consider creating a special promo code for each partner that helps their clients unlock a VIP upgrade or a BOGO buy one, get one bonus when they use your referral partner's custom promo code. This helps you track the referral and gives the buyer something special they will feel good about.

If you sell products, you may want to offer an extended warranty, free samples, free shipping, free delivery, free gift with purchase, or a gift card for future purchases.

If you sell services, you may want to offer a free upgrade to a premium service or solution.

You can always give a special discount for your partners in either a percentage or dollar amount. You might even offer free training, software, a magazine, or newsletter subscription to help them get better results with the service you provide. Just be sure to quantify the value they are receiving as a result of your referral partner's introduction.

Imagine all the special deals you'll be able to give your clients too. Claim this as a benefit they get when working with you and more people will come your way.

5 – Gift Certificates

There's no better price than free. That's why gift certificates are the ultimate way to package your special offer. Gift certificates allow your partners to recommend your services by giving their clients and customers something with high perceived value. While you may not want to give away your products and services for free, you can package a discount as a gift certificate to boost the perceived value. For example, if your average service costs $100, giving a $25 gift certificate is essentially a 25% discount.

Examples of gift certificates include:

- Mortgage loan officers offering a free credit report
- Realtors providing a free moving truck after closing
- Pool installation companies offering free lights with a new pool or spa
- Accountants offering a free tax return review
- Marketing consultants offering a free SEO audit
- Landscape maintenance companies offering one free month of service with a six or twelve-month agreement
- Private chefs offering a $50 gift certificate for any private party of eight or more
- Auto detailing companies offering a free VIP upgrade
- Home healthcare providers offering $100 in elderly care services

Simply print your gift certificates and include a brochure or flyer on your services for your referral partners to give to their clients. You may even want to have special gift certificate envelopes printed to create a special impression for your new clients.

6 – Consultations

If you provide consultations as part of your sales process, encourage your referral partner to include your service as part of theirs. Giving their clients a free consultation with you makes your referral partner look good and provides value to everyone involved.

Offering a free strategy session, discovery call, or consultation is also a great way to capture qualified leads that actually want to buy from your business. Not only do consultations help you capture more referrals, but you can streamline your sales process and add massive value by demonstrating your expertise in advance. This is especially effective for professional services and coaching businesses that thrive on establishing trusted relationships with their customers.

Consider creating a special landing page on your website or printing gift certificates or brochures that describe the service you provide to your partner's clients. Place a value on the assessment so the client understands they are getting something special thanks to your referral partner.

Depending on your industry, you may want to offer an alternative to a consultation. In that case, you may want to consider offering:

- Analysis
- Appraisals
- Assessments
- Audits
- Discovery Calls
- Estimates
- Evaluations
- Strategy Sessions

7 – Referral Cards

If you want to attract more *Raving Referrals*, it is imperative you make it easy for people to refer you. The fastest way to accomplish that is by giving people printed referral cards they can quickly hand to anyone who may need your products or services. This also helps you track where your business is coming from so you can recognize and reward your referrers.

You have probably received a referral card from your dentist, chiropractor, or home services professional. They are an inexpensive and effective way to help people help you. By including all the essential referral program information, these cards provide a simple way for people to refer others to your business.

One of the simplest ways to add a referral card into your business is by adding your referral offer to the back of your existing business card. You can also print a special postcard size promotional piece that gives people details about your product or service along with a special offer.

Be sure to include a catchy headline or slogan like:

- Refer a friend
- Help us spread the word
- Sharing is caring
- Friends wanted
- Pass it on
- Turn this card into cash
- A gift for you and your friends

Below the headline, include a call to action that gives people a reward for taking action. Offer a discount, free consultation, or special offer to make them feel special and increase the number of people who take advantage of your offer.

8 – Websites

Another great way to cross promote with your partners is by adding and recommencing them on your respective websites. Simply add them to a page that lists your resources, trusted partners, or preferred providers with links to their website or social media pages. Create a page on your site where your clients and customers can explore and connect with your trusted team of referral partners.

When creating a referral partner page of your website, list each partner with a sentence or two about the services they offer.

Display their contact information including phone number and website URL. Include their logo or banner ad linked to their website. If your partner offers special pricing or promotions, position that prominently so people know you are helping them unlock special pricing or treatment. You may also want to add a testimonial or success story from one of your clients or customers. Years ago, my company was a Preferred Supplier for Prudential Real Estate Affiliates, which was later purchased and rebranded as Berkshire Hathaway Home Services. Being listed on their website brought instant credibility to our company and led to hundreds of their Realtors joining our online referral program.

While many of their agents found us through the listing on their global Prudential corporate website, we also used the endorsement as a strategic partner when marketing to their agents directly. The credibility and visibility you gain when partners promote you on their website can be significant. Especially when you partner with influential brands and people.

9 – Social Posts

Social media is a powerful way to cross-promote with your partners. It's fast, easy, and free. When you combine forces and collaborate on Facebook, Instagram, Twitter, or LinkedIn, you reach new audiences creating instant credibility through the exposure and endorsement from your partner.

The key to this strategy is to coordinate a conversation by posting publicly. This creates an opportunity for your referral partners to answer, comment, and create a dialogue that others see and participate in. We recommend you pre-plan or at least coordinate what you and your partners are going to post so that both parties are promoted and provide value to your respective tribes of clients, fans, and followers. Some of the most effective ways to co-market with your partners include:

- **Success Stories** – Thank your partner publicly for helping clients get great results. Share the thanks you received from your clients for introducing your referral partners.
- **Testimonials** – Share your personal story of how impressed you've been by their knowledge, professionalism, and expertise. If you've personally used their product or service, share that as well to build social proof and trust.
- **Expert Content** – Provide special reports or whitepapers that educate people on your industry, products, or services.
- **Giveaways** – Offer to send free samples of your products or free trials of your service.
- **Special Offers** – Post discounts, promotions, or special offers.
- **Events** – Invite people to attend online or in-person events with you and your partners.
- **Questions and Quizzes** – Post questions about your partner's industry or area of expertise, tagging them to respond.
- **Photos and Videos** – Show before and after photos or videos to give visual examples of the impact you make.
- **Go Live** – Have a social conversation for the world to watch about anything from the list above.

10 – Newsletters

If you send out printed or email newsletters to your clients and prospect database, consider adding a section for your Referral Partners or top trusted pros. This adds value to your referral partners and shows you are committed to helping them win more clients. As you lead the partnership, they will feel indebted and want to return the favor either by giving you referrals directly or by cross-promoting you to their networks and social sphere. Just be sure to ask if they send out newsletters to their client list or database. If so, you can use any of the strategies above to cross-promote with your partners.

I've been using this strategy for over twenty years, and it is still as powerful today as it was back in the 1990's. Back then, my newsletter would feature mortgage loan programs and interest rates, as well as a segment thanking the Realtors, financial advisors, and other professionals who referred clients my way. I made sure each of my referral partners received my newsletter, so they felt appreciated for the business they sent. The real secret of this strategy was the social proof I manufactured by including the names of the people who trusted me enough to refer their clients and co-workers. As people saw the list of referral partners who trusted me, they gained confidence in my ability to deliver results which led them to start referring their best clients too.

11 – Team Brochures

As you start creating your trusted team of professionals, consider printing brochures featuring you and each of your referral partners. This gives both you and your partners a physical marketing tool you can share with your clients and display at your office or place of business. If you use this strategy, be sure all of the partners make a habit of giving these out to each new client you all have so everyone in your referral team is continuously promoting each other.

Team brochures work extremely well when you have a core group of professionals serving a specific target market or life event. Simply write an introduction as to the joint services and solution your team provides. Then list each partner including their name, company, logo, phone number, and website address. You may also want to include a brief statement or bulleted list of the specific services each partner provides.

12 – Bundled Offers

Another way to cross promote your partners is to actually bundle their services with your own. The way this strategy works is that you and your referral partner combine your services into one integrated solution or offer at a bundled price. You probably see this with travel companies who bundle airfare, hotel, car rental, and excursions into one bundled package. Mobile phone companies often bundle short-term subscriptions to music or movie applications with the purchase of a new phone in order to entice buyers and add extra value.

So how do you bundle your professional service with your referral partners? Just create an agreement whereby one partner sells the bundled service and pays the other partner to include their service in the bundle. For example, let's say you provide home cleaning services. Why not offer a spring cleaning or annual whole home special where you bundle carpet cleaning into the package. Or maybe you own an auto body shop. You might want to partner with an auto detailing company and clean your client's car before returning it to the client. Offering this VIP service package can help you stand out above your competition. This allows you to mark up what you charge for providing your services and brings a steady stream of new business.

This strategy can work for a lot of different professions. You just have to think creatively and out of the box. The more ways that you and your referral partners scout for new client opportunities for each other, the more business you will all have.

13 – Direct Mail

Once you are in agreement with your referral partners on a special offer, bundled service, or joint promotion you want to offer, sending your campaign through direct mail is a great way to get the word out. It gives your respective clients something tangible they can touch and feel forcing them to view your message and offer. When you utilize referred introductions and bundled offers into your direct mail campaign, you can leverage and maximize the results for both you and your referral partners.

While you may choose to mail your joint campaign to your respective client lists, you can also purchase or rent a list of *Perfect Prospects* you share with your partners. This allows you and your partners to target people in transitionary life events.

There are several top life events that cause people to search out new service professionals which you can target through direct mail campaigns including:

- New Homeowners
- New Car Buyers
- Engaged Or Just Married
- Expecting Or New Parents
- Retiring Or Recently Retired
- Divorcing Or Recently Divorced
- Moving Or Recently Moved

14 – Client Celebration Events

Events are a great way to bring people together and create new opportunities to connect. Consider hosting a quarterly or annual client celebration event with your referral partners. This can be as simple as hosting a happy hour at your office, or a local restaurant, bar, or hotel.

What's great about hosting these types of events with your referral partners is you can expand your audience while having fun celebrating great people. The key is to communicate to your referral partners the type of clients or professionals you would like them to invite so they fill the room with your perfect prospects.

As a reminder, some of the client appreciation events you can produce with your referral partners include:

- Art Showings
- Awards Parties: Oscars, Grammy's, Golden Globes
- Bowling Parties
- Casino Nights
- Charity Fundraising Events
- Cigar Nights
- Concerts
- Cornhole Tournaments
- Golf Tournaments
- Holiday Parties: Valentine's Day, Independence Day, Halloween, Thanksgiving, Christmas, New Year's Eve
- Private Movie Showings
- Sporting Events
- Top Golf Tournaments
- Wine Tours and Tasting

Be sure to capture everyone's contact information so you can follow up with them after the event to explore a relationship together.

15 – Sponsorships

If your referral partners already produce or participate in their own training events or conferences, you may want to consider sponsoring or exhibiting at their events. This shows your partners you support them and are committed to helping them achieve success. Sponsorship also creates opportunities for your referral partners to introduce or promote you and your services to their clients and strategic partners. You'll be amazed how many other partnership opportunities present themselves when you support your partners. The more you show up to help your partners in their passions and pursuits, the more they will recommend you and the services you provide.

In addition to sponsoring existing referral partners, you may want to sponsor:

- Association Events
- Bridal Expos
- Business Expos
- Chamber Of Commerce Events
- Charity Events
- Community Events
- Concerts
- Conferences
- Golf Tournaments
- Home And Garden Expos
- Networking Events
- Podcasts
- Races
- School Carnivals
- Sporting Events
- Trade Shows
- Webinars
- Websites

When considering a sponsorship opportunity, look to maximize exposure to your *Perfect Prospects*. If the event sponsor is gathering your ideal clients, the return on investment may justify the opportunity, especially since many event promoters will provide you the database of attendees as part of your sponsorship package.

Sponsorship benefits you should ask for include:

- Award Presentations
- Banner Ads on The Event Website and Mobile App
- Brochures Or Samples included in Attendee Gift Bags
- Direct Mail Campaigns
- Email Promotions before and after the Event
- Exhibitor Booth Space
- Logo Placement in Attendee Gift Bags
- Press Release
- Product Placement throughout the Event
- Signage throughout the Event
- Social Media Promotion
- Speaking Opportunities
- Tabletop Promotion
- VIP Sessions

16 – Workshops

As we discussed in chapter 11, workshops are a great way to educate people about the services you provide and the value you deliver. That's why you should talk to your partners about putting on a seminar, workshop, or lunch-and-learn training for your combined clients with each of you delivering a portion of the content. Just identify the top tips people need to know about the challenges you solve and how you help.

Training events help you attract qualified clients and boost your status as experts in your field. Once people have attended your class, they will understand why they need your service, and how you can help them solve their challenges and overcome their obstacles.

By establishing your expertise, you instantly elevate your status. Especially to those guests invited by your partners. There's simply no better way to gain the credibility and trust that gets transferred from the introduction of your referral partners. Plus, by mutually promoting the event to your respective clients, customers, fans, and followers, you leverage your combined audience to attract more profitable prospects.

If you produce the event and get your referral partners to promote it to their lists, you can expand your prospect database by capturing the contact information for all the people who register for the event. Then you can follow up with a variety of offers using your CRM or follow up system.

17 – Podcasts

Podcasts have grown in popularity and are now one of the best ways to establish yourself as an expert. Similar to a live workshop, podcasts give you an opportunity to interview your referral partners on their area of expertise. The strategy works just like a workshop, except rather than producing an in-person event, you simply record and broadcast your conversation much like a radio interview. Then you can post the audio file for people to listen to on their mobile device or computer. This allows them to download and listen to your conversation when it's most convenient for them.

Podcasts give you valuable content that both you and your referral partners can give away to prospects. You can also transcribe the recording and produce a special report your clients and social sphere can benefit from. The beauty of this strategy is that your referral partners will be happy to share the recording with their network because you are helping them boost their status and showcase their expertise. Just imagine how many referrals and leads you will attract when you get the right partners to promote your podcast to their audience because you have made them the star of the show.

Be sure to ask for a bio or some background on your referral partner so you can introduce them effectively. You may also want to research them on LinkedIn, their website, or social media to identify some interesting information to include in your conversation.

Here are some great questions you can ask during your podcast:

- How did you get started in your industry?
- What are the biggest challenges people come to you with?
- What is the most important thing you hope people learn from our conversation today?
- What would you say are the most common myths people have about your industry?
- What are some specific warning signs people should watch out for in your industry?
- What are you most proud of in your business?
- What are you most passionate about?
- Outside of work, what do you spend your time doing?
- What charities or social causes are you most passionate about?
- How has social media changed the way you do business?
- In your opinion, what is the future of...?

- How is technology impacting your industry?
- Tell me something that's true that almost nobody agrees with you on.
- How can people learn more about you and the solutions you provide?
- What's the best way for our listeners to connect with you?

We always recommend you give first and offer to interview your referral partners on your own podcast. This activates the law of reciprocity and will often lead them to return the favor. This strategy works powerfully when you interview people who already have significant social followings. Once the interview is over, offer to help them further by allowing them to interview you.

Just say, "*By the way, if it would be helpful, I would be happy to have you interview me so you have some content you can share with your audience.*" You will find they will be happy to return the favor, especially because they now feel indebted to you.

In addition to traditional podcasts, Clubhouse is a great platform for hosting audio interviews. Just download the Clubhouse app on your mobile phone and then start your own room or club. In a few short minutes, you can set up your own show that gets promoted to the Clubhouse community.

18 – Video Interviews

While audio podcasts are quick and easy to produce, video interviews via zoom and going live on social media are great ways to educate audiences about who and how you help. Before your interview, ask your partner what topics they want to cover and if they have any specific questions they would like you to ask. Then you can talk about the problems they solve and the solutions they provide.

Again, make sure they give you some background information so you can introduce them properly and establish their credibility. To prepare your partner, ask them to identify top tips people should know about their subject. This will give them confidence going into the interview and help you guide the conversation. Then ask the questions you've agreed to beforehand and invite any live viewers to ask any questions they have.

The video itself doesn't have to be a major Hollywood production. It can be a simple video shot on your mobile phone. Just do some testing and make sure the camera is steady, the lighting is good, and the audio is loud enough for your audience to hear clearly. You can shoot the video at one of your offices or out at a jobsite. If you can show visual examples of the work your referral partner does, even better.

Your goal is to give great content that helps your audience solve their challenges. Include a call to action at the end that makes it clear how to contact you and your referral partners should the person have questions or want to move forward.

19 – Webinars

Another way to present your expertise and attract clients for both you and your referral partners is by offering online webinars. The beauty of webinars is you can educate your audience and present your solutions far and wide. You can give presentations, perform product demonstrations, and deliver worldwide messages to thousands of people at a time. And if you create content that is informative and inspirational, you'll get great results and build a large list of prospects for your respective follow-up funnels.

Plus, because webinars are virtual, they save people from having to travel to attend your training in person and help you avoid the considerable costs of paying for meals or conference rooms to host live physical events.

To maximize the success of your webinar, follow these 10 steps:

1. **Choose a Topic** – Identify a topic that points out the pain points of your perfect prospects to inspire them to register for your training.
2. **Choose a Date and Time** – Select a time that works well for people locally and nationally if appropriate.
3. **Choose a Webinar Platform** – GoToWebinar, Zoom, and Webinar Jam are the platforms I've used and personally recommend.
4. **Invite Your Audience** – Both partners should text and email their databases and promote the event on your websites, blogs, and social media accounts.
5. **Build Your Content** – Create slides that identify the challenges you solve and spotlight the solutions and expertise each partner delivers.
6. **Practice** – Be sure to do a quick test run to ensure you're comfortable with the technology and that both speakers know which slides or sections each will be presenting.
7. **Host and Record Your Webinar** – Present your webinar as a masterclass, panel discussion, interview, case study, or product demo. Be sure to record it so you can post and share afterwards.
8. **Ask For Action** – Have a compelling call-to-action asking attendees to buy, try, or schedule a consultation to learn more.

9. **Follow-Up** – After your event, be sure to email, text, message, or call everyone who attended as well as those who registered but did not attend.
10. **Share Your Webinar Recording** – Post your webinar recording on your social media channels and email to your prospect and client database. You can even add the video to your website to provide ongoing education for your audience.

Some people choose to charge for their webinars, but if you're looking to attract a larger audience and build your prospect database, you should offer your class for free. This will give you the largest prospect list to follow up with after the webinar.

While you can sell products and services directly during your webinars, many people use webinars more to educate prospects who schedule a private consultation. Just be sure people feel the pain of not taking action, so they are motivated to move forward and learn more about the solutions you provide.

Landing the right promotional partner for your webinars can lead to hundreds or even thousands of *Perfect Prospects* being added to your sales funnel. One of our recent webinar campaigns attracted over 5,000 webinar registrants over a two-week period with over 2,000 people joining our live class. Rather than having to rent a conference center and incur the costs of producing an event of that size, we were able to host our event virtually which made it easy for everyone to attend.

20 – Referral Mixers

Hosting Referral Mixers is a fun and effective way to meet high quality professionals and prospects. When you host mixers, you become the central connector elevating your status as the leader of the group. Asking your top referral partners to co-host mixers helps you add value to your referral partners while you create a community of high-quality professionals.

Mixers provide the opportunity for people to meet in a festive and friendly atmosphere. Your role is simply to meet and introduce the people in your tribe. The more you help other people make new connections, the more your own network will grow.

This can easily be coordinated either at your office or a nearby restaurant, hotel, bar, or golf course. Once you know the location, date and time, you can start promoting the event using email, Eventbrite, Evite, a Facebook event, or other event invitation system. Then, enlist your referral partners to help get the word out by inviting their clients along with top professionals they know, like, and trust.

You can even target the event for a certain industry or group of professionals. Just be specific with your referral partners letting them know the types of people you are looking to attract so they fill the event with your *Perfect Prospects*. Then, when your mixer starts, you get to meet every single person who walks in the door as they check in at the registration table.

Best of all, you are meeting them from a position of prominence. You'll find them grateful for the invitation and impressed to meet the event producer bringing together so many fabulous people. The more you position yourself as a connector and catalyst, the more people will seek you out, asking how they can earn your trust and win your business.

If you live in a major market, you can always plug into existing networking events like those produced by Network After Work. They host events in over 80 major US markets typically bringing together over a hundred prominent professionals to each event. Strategically invite your referral partners to attend these events together with you. You will both increase your connections as you work the room together and introduce prospective referral partners and *Perfect Prospects* to each other.

21 – Charity Champion Campaigns

Personally, I love to partner with people to support charities and causes. You don't need to create your own charity to tap into the power of cause-related marketing. You can simply raise awareness, funds, and support for great causes and charities already doing good work.

Ask your referral partner if they have any charities or causes they support. If so, discuss how you might join forces and create more awareness and support for the causes that are near and dear to them. If you have a charity or organization you are passionate about, suggest that your referral partner join forces so you can create more impact together.

Some of the most fun and inspiring cause related marketing campaigns I've produced over the years include:

- **Christmas Kindness** – We produced a Christmas drive collecting toys, clothing, and canned food culminating with a concert and community celebration in Pioneer Square, the community courtyard in the center of downtown Portland. We gave points for each donation and awarded the top donation raiser a one-week trip to Cabo San Lucas, Mexico.

- **Virtual Veteran Salute** – We created VirtualSalute.com to honor U.S. veterans helping people nationwide post photos and share stories honoring the veterans in their lives.
- **We've Been Booed** – A fun and festive community-based campaign to spread joy before Halloween.
- **Donate Profit or Revenue** – One of my training companies donated 40% of our gross sales to charity partners who provided food, water, education and microloans in developing nations.
- **Empowerment Trainings** – We sent a volunteer team to lead the single largest private teacher training in the African nation of Liberia with the nation's President commencing over the day event.
- **Voluntour Trips** – We led volunteer teams overseas in Mexico and Africa as well as to South Dakota to build infrastructure for a Native American reservation.
- **Water Wells** – We helped drill water wells in Kenya.
- **Food Drives** – We helped produce the largest single food donation distribution day in the city of Los Angeles in partnership with Feed The Children led by Larry Jones and NBA legend Shaquille O'Neal.
- **Candle Wishes**– We supported a charity that provides birthday parties and gifts for underprivileged kids.
- **Toys For Tots** – We collected and donated toys for kids at Christmas.
- **Super V Pumpkin Shoot** – We created a 2-day competition hurling pumpkins hundreds of yards using roman catapults with all proceeds donated to Northwest Medical Teams.
- **Dog Rescues**– We regularly shelter, transport, and help dogs get rescued and adopted in the U.S. and Mexico.

These are some of my favorite give-back campaigns that have brought immense joy to me, my family, my employees, and my referral partners. While the business benefits are great, the personal satisfaction you get when you make a difference in the lives of others is immeasurable. There's simply nothing better than being a Charity Champion.

Each event creates an opportunity to invite your referral partners to participate and collaborate. Plus, when they see you as a leader committed to improving your community, they will want to do business with you for years to come. Whether you donate your time, talent, money, or promotion, everyone wins. Do more and give more for others and your life will be richly rewarded.

It Works When You Work It

These are the top 21 cross promotion campaigns you should consider implementing in your business. Hopefully you now see how using the *Referral Partner Blueprint* in your meetings with prospective and existing referral partners will help you have highly productive meetings that lead to profitable partnerships.

As you review each of the strategies, you will quickly gain clarity and agreement on what each person is willing to do for the other. Then as you put these 21 proven co-marketing campaigns to work in your businesses, you and your referral partners will be thrilled as you attract more client opportunities together.

Keep it simple. Start with the easiest campaigns you both feel most comfortable with and confident in. Then as you start seeing results and attracting more profitable prospects, you can implement additional co-marketing campaigns down the road at a later date.

Agree On Your Plan

As you and your referral partners sit down and create your *Referral Partner Blueprint*, be sure to agree on:

1. What each person will promote
2. When each partner will promote
3. How often each partner will promote

Print our handy checklist to use in your referral partner meetings. This will guide your conversation with prospective partners and help you both strategize the various ways you will cross promote each other.

Once your *Referral Partner Blueprint* is in place and you have agreed how each person or company will promote and refer the other, simply do what you committed to do, by the time you committed to do it, while your partner does the same.

Then, as the leads and new client opportunities start rolling in, be sure to thank them each and every time they generate another prospect for you. Provide regular updates on the status of each client they refer to you, so they know exactly how you are helping each of their clients. This will lead them to refer more clients because their appreciation for you will grow quickly. As we mentioned earlier, referral updates display a high level of professionalism, which continually build trust and will lead to further collaboration and opportunities together.

Your mutual clients will also tell your referral partners about how you've helped them. As your partners share success stories with other clients facing similar challenges, you will attract even more *Raving Referrals* for you and your firm.

Once you and your partners start actively referring and cross-promoting each other, you will find that your referrals and bottom line profits will increase steadily. You'll also develop some deep meaningful relationships with people you are proud to call your friends.

Co-marketing with your partners helps expand the visibility of your brand and the loyalty of your partners.

Scan this QR code or visit the link below for a quick video on how to get your message out to the masses through partners who proactively promote you to their best clients, customers and social sphere:

https://ravingreferrals.com/comarketing/

Time For ACTION

You are now empowered with the strategies, scripts, tips, and tricks you need to succeed. Everything you hope to accomplish can be achieved using the knowledge and wisdom you have in your hands. My question to you is, will you take the ACTION you need to win big?

The key to activating the Law of Attraction is taking MASSIVE ACTION. The more ACTION you take, the faster your business will grow. The good news is you can easily integrate what you've learned into your daily activities. With a few tweaks to what you already do, you can easily and effortlessly attract more *Perfect Prospects* and ideal clients.

As you start receiving *Raving Referrals*, we want to hear from you. Please take a moment and share your success story on our social channels. We'll reward you with a super-secret gift you'll be thrilled to receive.

Start now by sharing your AHA moments and breakthroughs right now. Just Scan the QR Code below using your mobile phone. You'll be glad you did.

Success Scripts

Scripts for Generating Raving Referrals

The following call and conversation scripts have been refined over decades of testing. Our goal is to give your clarity and confidence to help you generate *Raving Referrals* and profitable partnerships. Customize your conversations based on each person's **BANK**CODE and you will accelerate your results even faster.

Scripts or Building Reerral Partnerships:

Hi (name), the reason I'm calling is that I'm creating a team of professionals I'll be recommending to all my clients. I was thinking about you because I have a lot of clients who could benefit from your services. I'd love to sit down with you to discuss the possibility of adding you to my team and promoting you. When's a good time to get together and strategize?

Thanks so much for your time today. I'd like to ask for your help. As you may know, I am in the process of expanding my business and I'm looking for a great CPA to refer my clients to, so I'm wondering if you know of any good CPAs you think I should meet. I'm planning to meet and interview 2-3 and your CPA will be one of those I would like to meet with. Not just for my personal business, but also for the opportunity to refer clients to them. Is there anyone you'd recommend I meet with?

Stephen really sounds like an interesting person I would love to meet. Would you mind introducing the two of us? Or, if you would prefer, I am happy to send an email and mention you had great things to say about them and I would like to get to know them myself.

Thanks so much for the introduction. Would you be willing to make a quick call or send them a text to tell them how we know each other and that I will be calling them (date & time of scheduled call)? Is there anything you think I should know before I call them?

Thanks for meeting with me today. I've heard a lot of great things about you. You come highly recommended. The reason I wanted to meet with you is that I serve a lot of (type of client – homeowners/ business owners) who may be able to use your services. I'm hoping to learn more about you and your business so I'm referring you the right type of clients."

I'm glad to hear referrals are important to you. I work almost exclusively by referral which is exactly why I am here today. As I mentioned earlier, I'm looking for quality people I can partner with to grow our businesses together. Based on what you shared about your business, you are definitely the type of person I'm looking to add to my trusted team of professionals that I promote and refer my clients to.

Just to give you a little more background on me….

From what you've shared, I have a number of clients who might benefit from what you do. Can we get together another time so I can ask you a few questions? Maybe next Tuesday afternoon or Wednesday morning? What works best for you?

Hope all is well in your world. I'm reaching out because I am looking to expand my professional network and noticed you are connected to a few people on LinkedIn that I'd like to meet. I have a few contacts I think you would benefit from meeting as well. Do you have a few minutes to jump on a quick call so we can connect and collaborate? What day and time works best for your schedule?

Hi (name), As you may know, I am in the process of expanding my business and I'm creating an alliance of vetted and trusted professionals to refer my clients to. I truly value our relationship and would like to invite you to be a core member of my referral team. I will be gathering my most important referral partners (date/time) at (location) and hope you can attend. Please let me know if you can join us.

Referral Partner Alliance Meeting Script:

Thank you for coming today. The reason I asked you all to join me today is that I am expanding my business and I'm creating an alliance of vetted and trusted professionals to refer my clients to.

I truly value each and every one of you and view you as one of the best in your respective industries. Not only am I hoping to do more business with you personally, I also want to connect each of you so you can do more business together.

After all, everyone in this room serves (consumers/homeowners/business owners), so we share the same ideal client and can grow our businesses faster and further by cross-referring and cross-promoting each other.

What I'd like to do now is go around the room and give everyone a chance to introduce themselves and share who you help and how you help. That will help us all understand the services you provide and who your perfect prospects and ideal clients are.

I'll go first. As you all know, my name is ________________ and I help ________________________(share your Service Statement).

To give you an example of what I do, I recently had a client who____________________. (share a story of a problem you solved and the difference it made for them).

I'm passionate about helping people_______________and a great referral for me is a (share your Perfect Prospect Profile).

Before we move on, does anyone have any questions about the services I provide?

By the way, if it would be helpful, I would be happy to have you interview me so you have some content you can share with your clients/network/audience.

Scripts for Networking Events

The main reason I am here is that I'm looking for a quality (CPA) I can refer my clients to. Do you happen to know any good (CPA)s here you would recommend I connect with?

I'm wondering if you can help me. The primary reason I'm here is to find a top (CPA) that I can refer clients to and build a referral partnership with. Can you tell me if there are any quality (CPA)'s here I can connect with?

By the way, if you ever have a friend or family member you think might benefit from my services, I would be happy to meet with them at no charge to see how I might be able to help them.

Scripts to activate the Referral Triggers

I hope you're pleased with the service I've provided so far. Is there anything I can do to make you even happier?

Now that we've been working together for a while, I'm wondering if you can tell me what you have found most valuable about working with me?

I'm committed to growing my business through exceptional service. On a scale of 1-10, how happy would you say you are with my services?

Do you mind if I ask what you have liked best about working with me?

Thanks for sharing your feedback. Before you go, I'd like to ask you, if someone you know was asking about me or the services I provide, what would you tell them?

If you don't mind me asking, if you knew someone who was looking for a {insert your profession} how likely would you be to recommend me? What would you say?

Scripts to use when you hear the Referral Triggers

I'm so glad to hear that. I hope you'll recommend me any time you hear any *{describe your Perfect Prospect}* mention that they are looking for a good *{insert your profession}* or need help *{share your Service Statement}*. Is there anyone who comes to mind who might need my help?

I'm so glad you feel that way. I love helping clients like you *{share your Service Statement}*. By the way, I may have mentioned before that I am expanding my business so if you know any *{describe your Perfect Prospect}* who might need help *{share your Service Statement}*, I'd love to connect with them and see if I can help them the way I helped you?

Do you know anyone who is looking to *{share your Service Statement}?*

Scripts for Asking Clients for Referrals

Thanks for meeting with me today. Before you leave, I'd like to ask for your help. As you may know, I am in the process of expanding my business and one of the ways I keep my costs down is by working primarily by referral, so I don't have to spend much time or money on advertising. Once I've taken care of you and hopefully have exceeded your expectations, I'd like to ask your permission to ask you for referrals. Would that be all right?

As you may know, I prefer working with people who are referred to me/us. Right now, I'm giving a special discount to friends or family of our existing clients. If there's anyone you'd like to refer to me, they will get an extra 10% off our premier package *(customize with your offer)*. And of course, I'll take extra special care of them since they're coming from you. Is there anyone you can think of who might like to take advantage of this?

As you know, nearly all of my business comes from referrals. A good referral for me is *{describe your Perfect Prospect}* who might need help *{share your Service Statement}*. Of everyone you know, who would be the best referral for me? Why do you say that?

As you know, nearly all of my business comes from referrals. I'm hoping we can brainstorm for a few minutes to see if we can identify some people you care about who should at least know about the work we do and the process we use to help people. Would that be alright?

Great. Please let me know if there's anyone you know I can help. I'm always here for you and your clients.

Congratulations on completing the *Raving Referrals* book. You now have the proven strategies, scripts, tips, and tricks you need to succeed. Scan this QR code or visit the link below for a quick video on the #1 most important driver for success in attracting *Raving Referrals*:

https://ravingreferrals.com/completion/

Experts & Influencers

When it comes to expanding the social reach of your business or brand, nothing matches the credibility and visibility you can gain from partnering and cross-promoting with experts and influencers. If you are looking for a podcast guest, joint venture partner, industry expert, best-selling author, keynote speaker, advisor, or board member, these are the people we highly recommend as some of the best in business:

Aaron Young – Chairman of Laughlin Associates

Aaron serves as Chairman of Laughlin Associates, a 44-year old company that has helped over 100,000 entrepreneurs start, grow, and profit from their business by providing fast, easy and reliable business incorporation and LLC formation services. This perspective has given Aaron an ideal vantage point to observe common mistakes and successes in businesses from Main Street to America's largest yacht broker, from medical professionals to manufacturers to investors. For over 34 years, his experience founding, acquiring and directing multi-million-dollar businesses as well as working as an officer for a publicly traded, multi-national, sets him apart from the crowd as a voice of real-world knowledge and authority.

AaronScottYoung.com

Adrian Chenault – CEO of Contact Mapping

Adrian Chenault is the CEO and Co-Founder of Contact Mapping, a powerful way to turn your network into a priceless resource. Contact Mapping creates a smart layer on top of your contacts that makes it easy for you to remember the most important details about your connections, reminds you when it's time to get in touch, and allows you to "Google your own memory" to find anyone based on anything. In addition, Adrian is the Amazon #1 Bestselling author of "The Coffee Shop Interview", a guide on having exceptional business conversations.

ContactMapping.com/free

Allison H Larsen – Founder of The Speakers Coalition

Allison H Larsen is an intuition expert and author of the book "Soul Intuition". As the Founder of The Speakers Coalition and Co-Founder of Legendary, she has been featured on stages, media, and virtual platforms all over the world. She has received multiple awards for her work, including the Achievement in Excellence Award from the City Summit Foundation. Allison has worked with thousands of clients over the past decade to help them increase their intuition and their reach. Her clients have included professional athletes, Olympians, and well-known thought leaders. She is especially passionate about working with up-and-coming speakers and intuitive entrepreneurs to help them increase their influence and income.

TheSpeakersCoalition.com

Ann DeVere – Executive Producer of Access to Experts TV

Ann DeVere is a global visibility catalyst and is the executive producer of "Access to Experts" and "Meet The Press LIVE". She is an international speaker, trainer and consultant who is committed to helping people expand their visibility and credibility. Whether you want to be interviewed on network TV, or you want to be an influencer on social media, Ann is the "Go-To-Expert" if you want to share your WHY TEDx style on camera so you can strategically showcase your expertise to attract your divine clients.

AccessToExperts.com

Barbara Wainwright – CEO of Wainwright Global

Barbara Wainwright is a Certified Master Life Coach and CEO of Wainwright Global. She is known as the most sought-after teacher in the life coaching and self-empowerment industry. She is famous for training and certifying over 6,500 professional coaches worldwide since 2006 and for empowering individuals to actualize their life purpose, live inspired lives, and connect with their true passion. Barbara is an international speaker, author and trainer and now has three books available on Amazon.com.

LifeCoachTrainingOnline.com

Becky Norwood – CEO of Spotlight Publishing

Becky's sought-after publishing house guides authors to reach hearts by weaving storytelling into the pages of the books they bring to the world. Having brought over 300 authors to #1 bestseller, she masterfully guides them to use their books as tools for business growth, sharing the mindset, tool sets and systems for success.

SpotlightPublishing.pro

Beejel Parmar – Co-Founder of The Process Hive

If you want practical ways to overcome overwhelm, defeat distractions, and punch procrastination in the face, you'll want to connect with Beejel Parmar. With over a decade of experience helping entrepreneurs and businesses boost their productivity and outsourcing their busy work to virtual assistant services, you'll soon be making a beeline towards saving time and getting the best things done.

BeelineProgram.com

Burke Franklin - CEO and Founder
BusinessPowerTools.com

You're starting or building a business... How do you handle the everyday challenges of organizing, planning, funding, managing, marketing, policies, procedures, sales... and everything else?

BusinessPowerTools.com is a collaborative business toolbox that has evolved over 30 years with hundreds of customizable software templates for startups, growing companies and their advisors. Along the way, Burke was elected to the White House Conference on Small Business and was nominated for Ernst & Young's "Entrepreneur of the Year" award. His book, "Business Black Belt", helps entrepreneurs build their own companies and apply lessons from 40+ years of personal development workshops, martial arts, flying, and real-world business success.

BusinessPowerTools.com
BurkeFranklin.com

Carol Dysart – Founder of People Smart Enterprises

Carol is a DISC profiling master who has been consulting and mentoring business owners and leaders for over three decades. Her superpower is helping others apply her People Smart communication skills for singles, couples, families, small business owners, and CEO's in corporations of any size. Her mastery comes from her many years of experience and training in the personality science of the DISC model for "*understanding self and others.*"

CarolDysart.com
PeopleSmartAcademy.com

Casey Eberhart – The Ideal Networker

Casey Eberhart is a master of networking and follow-up systems. Having served as the emcee at the world's most elite marketing event, Traffic & Conversion Summit, Casey knows firsthand that knowledge is not what's holding people back... it's the implementation of the right strategies. As a keynote speaker and trainer, Casey has been helping entrepreneurs and business owners for over three decades building multiple 7-figure businesses in the process. Casey teaches the fundamental art and science of connectivity, lead generation, lead conversion, and customer experience. When you master these 4 business skills, you can be dropped anywhere in the world and network your way to success.

CaseyEberhart.com

Cheri Tree – CEO of Codebreaker Technologies

Cheri Tree is a best-selling author, professional keynote speaker, and world-renowned entrepreneur. She is the founder and CEO of Codebreaker Technologies, with clients in more than 100 countries worldwide.

She is the creator of the revolutionary **B.A.N.K.** methodology and Codebreaker's Personality Coding Technology, designed to help business owners close more sales in less time and improve their communication skills and personal relationships. Cheri has spoken to hundreds of thousands of entrepreneurs and professionals globally at some of the top business conferences in the world.

CodebreakerTech.com

Cory Michael Sanchez – Co-Founder of Mojo Global

Cory Michael Sanchez is one of the top paid traffic experts in the country. His company, Mojo Global, has helped clients book over 1 million appointments and helped customers generate over $100M in revenue with customers in 30+ countries. Entrusted to run the advertising campaign for the largest Marketing Event in North America, he is exceptional at driving high converting traffic for brands that need exposure, funding, and new clients.

Featured in Forbes, he and his business partner Ira Rosen are considered to be top 1% influencers in the world by LinkedIn Corporation and has trained 100,000's of entrepreneurs just like you how to create predictable leads, clients and revenue. Winners of the prestigious "Marketer of the Year" award through the Phoenix Business Journal, they will show you how to tap into paid media to drive affordable traffic to your brand and company.

mojoglobal.com

Craig Shelley – COO of IMPACT Realty Tampa Bay

If you are searching for seasoned leadership in the real estate industry, look no further than Craig Shelley. After a career spanning more than 40 years as a business building executive, including eight years as a vice president of RE/MAX International and five years as Regional President of EXIT Realty Corp. International in Colorado and Utah, Craig now serves as C.O.O. of IMPACT Realty Tampa Bay, a thriving real estate brokerage making waves in the Florida market. Craig holds an MBA-International Business degree from the Thunderbird School of Global Management and is passionate about leading the next generation of leaders. Craig's public speeches regularly produce laughter, tears, and standing ovations. The fact that he comfortably conducts business in English, Spanish, and Portuguese only expands his influence and impact.

IMPACTRealtyTampa.com

Cynthia Kersey – Unstoppable Philanthropist

Cynthia Kersey is the best-selling author of two books, "Unstoppable", and "Unstoppable Women", an international speaker, entrepreneur, and Founder & CEO of the Unstoppable

Foundation whose mission is to ensure that every child has access to a quality education. Cynthia knows firsthand that giving is not only good for the soul, but also for business. She provides business owners with a practical action plan on how they can expand their business, create customer evangelists, and become completely invigorated about their life and business by integrating generosity as a business philosophy.

UnstoppableFoundation.org

Danny Creed – Hall of Fame Business Coach

Danny Creed is a master business coach and turnaround expert who has been advising executives, business owners, entrepreneurs and sales professionals for over 15 years. He has been personally coached and mentored by the legendary Brian Tracy and is the six-time recipient of the FocalPoint International Brian Tracy Award of Sales Excellence, and the 2019 FocalPoint Coaching Practice of the year. Some of his marquee clients include ON Semiconductor, Freedom Financial, AVNET, XEROX, and SRP. In addition to coaching, Danny also delivers powerful keynote and workshop presentations to audiences worldwide at corporate events and conferences. He is a published author of six business and motivational books, including the bestseller "CHAMPIONS NEVER MAKE COLD CALLS."

RealWorldBusinessCoach.com

Dave Savage – CEO of Mortgage Coach

Dave Savage, the co-founder of Mortgage Coach, is an innovator and change agent known in the mortgage industry for reinventing how loan officers quote rates and turn mortgage advice into a competitive advantage. Dave transforms originators into Black Belt Mortgage Advisors with high-tech, and high-trust strategies and tactics. He is passionate about innovating sales training with a combination of video and YouTube; the Mortgage Coach YouTube channel is hailed as "Netflix" for loan officers.

MortgageCoach.com

David Baer – Marketing Strategist

David Baer is a marketing expert who works with professional services businesses, like financial advisors, to design a customized roadmap with strategies and systems to make sure they take advantage of every possible opportunity to add revenue. David is especially adept at showing his clients where they can find money they've been overlooking that's often hiding right in front of them.

ThePreparedGroup.com

David Fagan – Best-Selling Speaker, Author, Expert

David T. Fagan is the former CEO of Guerrilla Marketing and is best known for his authority marketing, content creation, and talent management skills in the world of publishing, publicity, and presentations. David and his team of experts live to support and promote the expert talent they represent.

DavidTFagan.com

David Meltzer – Cofounder of Sports 1 Marketing

David Meltzer is the Co-Founder of Sports 1 Marketing and formerly served as CEO of the renowned Leigh ("Lee") Steinberg Sports & Entertainment agency, which was the inspiration for the movie "Jerry Maquire." David has been recognized by Variety Magazine as their Sports Humanitarian of the Year and awarded the Ellis Island Medal of Honor. He is also the Executive Producer of the Bloomberg and Amazon Prime television series "2-Minute Drill" and "Office Hours." His life's mission is to empower OVER 1 BILLION people to be happy! This simple yet powerful mission has led him on an incredible journey to provide one thing...VALUE. In all his content, and communication that's exactly what you'll receive. As part of that mission, for the past 20 years, he's been providing free weekly trainings to empower others to empower others to be happy.

Dmeltzer.com

Debbie Allen – Best-Selling Author of The Highly Paid Expert

Debbie Allen, aka 'The Experts of the Experts,' is an expert positioning business mentor, professional speaker and a best-selling author or nine books including,"The Highly Paid Expert" and "Success is Easy."

Debbie hosts online and live events, has multiple online courses and hosts her podcast Access to Experts.

DebbieAllen.com

Dennis Doran – Author of Soft as Steel

As a leading expert in the construction industry with more than forty years of experience, Dennis Doran delivers powerful, actionable lessons about people and services with high energy and humor. While he comes from a storied career in the construction industry, his content delivers a critical competitive advantage for anyone in any field. As the author of "*Soft as Steel*", he equips people with the tools to be successful, not just in business, but in life and relationships. As a speaker, trainer and certified facilitator of Extreme Leadership, Dennis teaches people how to take the Radical LEAP and lead with love, empathy, audacity, and proof.

DennisDoranSpeaking.com

Earl Kemper – Master Business Coach

Over the past 33 years, Earl has coached more than 1,400 business owners, who on average, double profits in their business within 36 months. Earl is an authority on developing strategic alliances and referrals. He helps his clients achieve more with less by increasing their sales, profits, and most importantly helping them achieve the vision they have for their business and life. The client results he has generated have led him to twice be recognized as the ActionCOACH Global Coach of the Year where he ranks as the #1 coach when ranked by the results of this clients. Now he specializes in helping financial advisors and dental practice owners increase both revenue and profit.

EarlKemper.com

Elias Zepeda – CEO of Need Clients NOW

Elias Zepeda is the founder and CEO of Need Clients Now, a national marketing agency specializing in customer acquisition. Throughout the years, Elias and his team have been helping businesses small and large scale by building their high-converting sales funnels for their businesses in various industries.

NeedClientsNow.com

Emily Letran – High Performance Dental Coach

Dr. Emily Letran is most proud of being known as the "Best Mom in the World!" As a certified high-performance coach and marketing strategist, she helps dentists, business professionals and entrepreneurs increase their net income, decrease stress, position themselves as authority figures, create social impact, and enjoy happy, fulfilling lives through her coaching programs.

DrEmilyLetran.com

Emmeline Saavedra – President of The Champions Institute

As the President of The Champions Institute, Emmie is committed to creating a world where champions lead with courage, love, and excellence. As the #1 global Certified **BANK**CODE Trainer, Emmie and her team train and coach businesspeople to optimize their people, processes and profits creating more income, influence and impact. The Champions Institute provides transformative sales and leaderships programs that empower people to achieve their purpose, performance and prosperity transforming them into Champions both personally and professionally.

TCIChampions.com

Eric Lofholm – CEO of Eric Lofholm International Eric

Eric Lofholm is the President and CEO of Eric Lofholm International, a company he founded to provide professional sales training. Since 1999, he has trained over 10,000 salespeople and entrepreneurs his proven sales strategies. When Eric started in sales, he was a bottom producer for an entire year and was nearly fired for not hitting his quota. It was at that point Eric got professionally trained. The next month he hit quota and the following month he became the top producer in his company. He has written 3 main books including *"Sales Scripting Mastery"* one of the most comprehensive books ever written on sales scripting. Eric lives in Rocklin, California with his wife Heather and his 4 children.

EricLofholm.com

Gail Watson – CEO Women Speakers Association

Gail Watson is the Founder and CEO of Women Speakers Association (WSA), the go-to place for innovative leaders, change agents and women with a message. WSA provides a platform for women to get seen, booked, and paid and be part of a global network reaching women in 120 countries. Whether her "stage" be a classroom, boardroom, or the floor of the UN, Gail is dedicated to empowering women to authentically express themselves and build a thriving, prosperous business.

WomenSpeakersAssociation.com

Gelie Akhenblit – Networking Guru

Gelie is the CEO and Founder of NetworkingPhoenix.com. It is the largest professional organization in Phoenix, AZ with over 40,000 members. Gelie consults business owners on strategic business development and relationship marketing, as well as facilitates high-level warm introductions and runs influence marketing campaigns through her own media channels. A seasoned presenter, one of Gelie's favorite accolades was being invited to share her message on a TEDx stage. As her tagline goes, "Who do you want to meet? I'll introduce you."

Gelie.com

Greg Hague – Founder & CEO OF 72SOLD.COM

If you live in Phoenix AZ, you know who Greg Hague is. He's on your TV sharing how you can sell your home to 72Sold.com for a higher price in 72 hours. You can even stay in your home up to 6 months after you sell. You see his bright 72Sold digital billboards along all the most trafficked freeways in the city. What you may not know is that this brilliant man once earned the top score on the Arizona bar exam and has now committed himself to helping people avoid the hassle of selling their home the old-fashioned way. Beyond business, this world traveler has been attacked by a bear, crashed his motorcycle in Africa, force-landed his plane on a remote island in the Atlantic, and raced Porsches. Of all his adventures, he claims "the most rewarding is improving the way America sells homes with 72SOLD... and marrying Teresa, the most remarkable girl in the world."

72sold.com

Greg Reid – Founder of Secret Knock

For over 25 years, Greg Reid has inspired millions of people to take personal responsibility and step into the potential of their greatness. His books, "Stickability: The Power of Perseverance," "The Millionaire Mentor," and "Three Feet from Gold: Turn Your Obstacles into Opportunities," have inspired countless readers to understand the most valuable lessons we learn, are also the easiest ones to apply. Greg is best known for being the founder of Secret Knock, which both Forbes and Inc. magazines rate as one of the top global events for partnership, networking, and business development. In addition to producing the Oscar qualified film, Wish Man, based on the creator of the Make A Wish Foundation, Greg has himself been honored with a star of the infamous Las Vegas Walk of Stars.

GregReid.com
SecretKnock.co

Harrison Rogers – CEO of HJR Global

Harrison Rogers is a serial entrepreneur and investor who is passionate about turning ideas into lucrative ventures. In 2012, he launched Lexington Learning Center which provides special needs care, providing services for autism education, emotional disabilities and behavioral health support through both in-center and in-home care. This company ranked as one of the fastest growing companies in America. Harrison is an active real estate investor owning numerous residential and commercial properties and management companies. Harrison is also a tech investor and has been voted Most Influential in Valley Business two years in a row, Arizona Republic's 35 under 35 and Phoenix Magazine's 40 under 40.

HJRGlobal.com

Itamar Shafir – CEO Umbrella Micro Enterprises

tamar is the Founder & CEO of Umbrella powering 2500 marketers globally. Formally the founder and CEO of Appforma, an award-winning automated marketing platform (acquired by Algomizer), B2B SaaS entrepreneur and investor. Itamar is and expert SSMB SaaS, MarTech, Marketing, GigEconomy and Business Opportunity leader.

Umbrellaus.com

Ivan Misner – Founder of BNI Business Network International

Dr. Ivan Misner is the Founder of BNI. Today, the organization has over 10,000 chapters on every populated continent of the world. He is a New York Times bestselling author who has written 26 books. He has been featured in the L.A. Times, Wall Street Journal, and New York Times, as well as the BBC and The Today Show on NBC. Dr. Misner has been called the "Father of Modern Networking" by CNN and one of the "Top Networking Experts" in the world by Forbes. He is considered by most, to be one of the world's leading authorities on the topic. In addition, the John C. Maxwell organization recently named him the "Transformational Leader of the Year."

IvanMisner.com

James Miller – CEO of Network After Work

James Miller is the Founder and CEO of Network After Work, America's premier face-to-face business networking company which he launched in 2009. In its peak, the organization produced monthly mixer events in over 85+ cities catering to over 6 million members. Network After Work quickly became the largest and fastest growing organization of its kind. Recently, the organization expanded and now offers virtual networking events along with empowering content delivered by world-class trainers and experts. James and his team are always looking for experts they can feature to their network.

NetworkAfterWork.com

Jay Fiset – Joint Venture Expert

Jay Fiset is a best-selling author, student of human nature, and founder of JVology. He is a member of the ClickFunnels Two Comma Club, has built multiple 7-figure businesses, and is creating a groundbreaking business relationship-building platform driven by Artificial Intelligence. Jay mentor's clients on creating profitable joint ventures and also serves as a global speaker and high-ticket sales expert with a unique perspective on business growth that mixes people, fun, and profit.

JVology.com

Jeff Brain – CEO of CloutHub

Have you ever dreamed of creating your own social media platform where people can connect and collaborate? Where voices can be heard, and authentic expression is allowed? That's what Jeff Brain envisioned when he set out to create CloutHub, a social network designed for meaningful civic, social and political engagement. Existing social media platforms have transformed commerce, relationships and business. What is missing Is a platform that brings people together and enables them to access information and tools that enrich their lives and makes the world and society better. Jeff is on a mission to bring people together to connect, socialize and impact the issues they care about and CloutHub connects them to what matters most in their lives. Protecting freedom of expression, member privacy, and member health. CloutHub is the future of social media!

CloutHub.com

Jeff Hoffman – Chairman of Global Entrepreneurship Network

Jeff Hoffman is a proven CEO, a successful serial entrepreneur (Priceline.com/Booking.com, and uBid.com). Jeff is a worldwide motivational speaker, producer of a Grammy-winning jazz album, executive producer of an Emmy-winning TV show, and mentor to entrepreneurs and startups all over the world. Jeff's passion for transforming the world through business has led him to serve as Chairman of the Global Entrepreneurship Network (GEN) which works in 200 countries, connecting entrepreneurs, investors, researchers, and policymakers to build one global entrepreneurial ecosystem.

JeffHoffman.com

GenGlobal.org
jeff@jeffhoffman.com

Jeffrey Hayzlett – CEO of C-Suite Network

Jeffrey Hayzlett is a global business celebrity Hall of Fame speaker, best-selling author, and Chairman & CEO of the C-Suite Network, home of the world's most trusted network of C-Suite leaders. Jeffrey is a well-traveled public speaker, former Fortune 100 CMO, and author of four bestselling business books: "The Hero Factor," "Think Big, Act Bigger: The Rewards of Being Relentless, Running the Gauntlet," and "The Mirror Test." As a leading business expert, Hayzlett is frequently cited in Forbes, SUCCESS, Mashable, Marketing Week and Chief Executive, among others. Jeffrey shares his executive insight and commentary on television networks like Bloomberg, MSNBC, Fox Business, and C-Suite TV. Hayzlett is a former Bloomberg contributing editor and primetime host. He is a turnaround architect of the highest order, a maverick marketer and c-suite executive who delivers scalable campaigns, embraces traditional modes of customer engagement, and possesses a remarkable cachet of mentorship, corporate governance and brand building.

C-SuiteNetwork.com

Jerry Conti – CEO of BoomSTR

Jerry is a serial entrepreneur, humanitarian, community leader and world-class connector. As the Vacation Rentals LLC, "LuxHomePro", and LuxHomePro Holdings LLC, Jerry's primary focus is helping real estate investors build wealth through short-term rentals which he does through BoomSTR.com, and a Digital Marketing Agency for short term rentals. As an expert in the field of strategic partnerships, Jerry loves learning, collaborating with incredible people and spending time with his wife Jessica and 14-year-old son Jayden.

BoomSTR.com
JerryConti.com
LuxHomePro.com

Jesse Doubek – CEO of Influencer Technologies

Jesse Doubek is one of the most successful online marketers of our time. As Founder and CEO of Influencer Technologies, his unique spin on the way influencers need to develop their businesses and marketing strategies, has led to the opportunity to work with some of the greatest online entrepreneurs in the world, including NYT Bestselling Authors like Brendon Burchard, Chalene Johnson, Sharon Lechter, and Sonia Choquette. By combining the know-how of his done-for-you marketing agency (Influencer Digital), with InfluencerSoft, the innovative software that helps influencers grow their businesses faster, and adding in the top-notch mentoring and coaching that all business owners need through the Influencer Mentoring Division, he has developed a completely unique and highly successful way for influencers to make their significant impact on the world.

InfluencerSoft.com

Jill Lublin – PR Guru

Jill Lublin is an international speaker on the topics of radical influence, publicity, networking, kindness and referrals. She is the author of four Best Selling books including, "Get Noticed... Get Referrals," (McGraw Hill), and co-author of "Guerrilla Publicity" and "Networking Magic." Her latest book, "Profit of Kindness," went #1 in four categories. Jill is a master PR strategist on how to position your business for more profitability and more visibility in the marketplace. Jill teaches a virtual Publicity Crash Course and consults and speaks all over the world. She also helps authors to create book deals with major publishers and agents, as well as obtain foreign rights deals.

PublicityCrashCourse.com/freegift
Jill_Lublin.com

Jim Canfield – Best Selling Author of CEO Tools 2.0

Jim Canfield is a CEO coach, strategic consultant, internationally awarded speaker and author of CEOTools 2.0 How to Think, Lead and Manage Like a CEO. He is one of the top thought leaders on ways CEOs and teams can communicate, execute, and optimize their businesses more efficiently and effectively.

CEOTools.com

John Jantsch – Best-Selling Author of Duct Tape Marketing

John Jantsch is a marketing consultant, speaker, and author of "Duct Tape Marketing," "The Referral Engine," "The Self-Reliant Entrepreneur," and "The Ultimate Marketing Engine." He is also the founder of the Duct Tape Marketing Consultant Network, which trains and licenses independent consultants and agencies to use the Duct Tape Methodology.

DuctTapeMarketing.com

Julianne O'Connor – Dental High-Performance Trainer

Julianne O'Connor helps high-achieving CEOs and dentists leverage their influence and prioritize quality of life. She is an award-winning author, actor, TEDx speaker, brand strategist, Certified Strategic Intervention Coach and Certified Corporate Trainer with a focus on work-life balance, burnout prevention, careers, new product launches, branding and up-levelling influence. Julianne also provided powerful strategies for growth, led by "quality of life" and "burnout prevention" coaching. She also provides dentists and their teams with powerful strategies for effective branding and done-for-you social media packages.

SpellingItOut.com

Kim Marie Branch-Pettid – CEO of LeTip

After spending 28 years in the banking industry specializing in mergers and acquisitions, Kim Marie purchased LeTip and has spent the past 20 years leading and expanding the business-building organization across North America. She is passionate about empowering business owners and professionals with the tools, training, and technology they need to succeed. With thousands of members in over 250 chapters, Kim Marie is committed to helping people create powerful and profitable strategic alliances and referral partnerships. She is also heavily involved in organizations, associations, and charities that support entrepreneurs, women in business, and children.

LeTip.com

Kristine Vowles – Celebrity Interior Designer

Kristine is the founder of The Luxury Look, an award-winning international design firm that specializes in transforming spaces and adding beauty to every project and property. Having viewed thousands of homes and estates over her two decades in real estate sales, Kristine specializes in interior design for luxury estates, vacation homes, and investment properties. She operates under a strict privacy agreement, so celebrities and executives are safe in her creative hands.

TheLuxuryLook.com

Kyle Fuller – Infinite Banking Authority

One thing that is certain for Kyle Fuller is the Infinite Banking Concept is not a career or business, he considers it his calling in life. He has no plans to retire as he plans to educate families and business owners about Infinite Banking until the day he graduates from this life. If you are ready to be the bank and take advantage of the financial strategies used by the biggest banks on the planet, or would like to teach this to your clients or community, reach out to Kyle at:

FactumFinancial.com

Lisa Patrick – Business Strategist

Lisa Patrick is the modern-day Nancy Drew of business working to help busy high performers get clarity and the right resources to take their ideas and thought leadership to market and scale. For over 20 years, Lisa has built her pedigree as a startup specialist, award-winning podcast host of "Coffee with Lisa," managing partner at Assessments24x7.ca, co-founder of Belongify, contributor at Entrepreneur and Forbes, speaker and co-author of, "Intelligent Curiosity." Having worked alongside some of the most influential thought leaders in the world of professional speakers and the c-suite makes Lisa one of the most sought-after startup consultants and branding experts by professionals.

LisaPatrick.ca
Belongify.com

Lynn Rose – CEO of WowMaker

Lynn Rose is an award-winning media and entertainment entrepreneur, business consultant and Founder/CEO of WOWMAKER: the first ever positive social media platform designed to drive personal, professional and global change (launching to 100's of millions on release). She's shared the stage and/or screen with Stevie Wonder, Meryl Streep, Ashton Kutcher, Halle Berry, Mariah Carey, Arnold Schwarzenegger, Tony Robbins, Deepak Chopra and countless other luminaries, and been seen on CBS, ABC, NBC, film and more. Behind the scenes, she's worked with billion-dollar CEOs, thought leaders, and experts. Her access to celebrities, Fortune 500 companies, and well-known influencers brings together brands, celebrities, influencers, and everyday people within an all-in-one hub for collaborating and activating good together: for ourselves and the world. For the leading solutions and brands that the world needs, this innovative platform acts as an all-in-one engine for business helping them reach the masses in a meaningful way, while getting to be part of positive global impact.

WowMakerNow.com

Mark Victor Hansen – World's #1 Best Selling Non Fiction Author

Mark Victor Hansen is an enthusiastic crusader of what's possible and is driven to "make the world work for 100 percent of humanity." He is best known as the co-author for the "Chicken Soup for the Soul" book series, setting world records in book sales with over 500 million books sold. Mark is also a sought-after keynote speaker, and entrepreneurial marketing maven, creating a stream of successful people who have created massive success for themselves through Mark's unique teachings and wisdom. With his endearing charismatic style, Mark captures his audience's attention as well as their hearts. Having spoken to over 6000 audiences worldwide with his one-of-a-kind technique and masterful authority of his work, he continues to receive high accolades from his audiences as one of the most dynamic and compelling speakers and leaders of our time. Mark has been featured on television (Oprah, CNN and The Today Show), print (TIME, US News & World Report, USA Today, The New York Times and Entrepreneur) and countless radio and newspaper interviews as he assures people everywhere that "with the right principles and mentors, you can easily create the life of your dreams." Mark believes you have a book in you and is committed to helping people publish their stories to create new opportunities and leave a lasting legacy.

MarkVictorHansen.com

Michela Quilici – International Business Navigator

Michela Quilici is an international business growth coach, award-winning marketing strategist, Amazon bestselling author, speaker, Forbes coach, Predictable Profits® growth consultant, and Global Operations and Training Director at Women Speakers Association.

As a "Business Navigator", Michela works with growth-minded business owners and CEOs who seek better marketing, sales, and revenue systems for more predictability, profitability, and scalability in any economy. She helps her clients accelerate and navigate their business growth on purpose, using strategy, systems, and self-leadership.

MichelaQuilici.com

Mike Keeter – Dental Business Development Expert

Mike Keeter is a growth expert who works at the very top of the dental implant industry. After earning the distinction and award of achieving the #1 top national new customer development specialist for Nobel BioCare, Mike doubled down on his commitment to empowering dentists to learn and adopt leading oral surgical technologies alongside industry leading experts from around the world. Mike leads educational courses that cover everything from dental diagnosis and treatment planning to surgical and prosthetic processes. Mike even addresses complex and progressive protocols for managing potential complications.

MikeKeeter.com

Noah St. John – Peak Performance Success Coach

Noah St. John is known as "The Millionaire Habits Coach" and the founder of SuccessClinic.com, a global peak performance and business growth company. Noah has worked with 8+ figure company CEOs and individuals since 1997. His clients have added more than $2.7 Billion dollars in sales by following his legendary methods. Noah is the only author in history to have works published by HarperCollins, Hay House, Simon & Schuster, Mind Valley, Nightingale-Conant, and the Chicken Soup for the Soul publisher.

He has appeared on over 1,000 media outlets including ABC, NBC, CBS, Fox, The Hallmark Channel, NPR, PARADE, SUCCESS, Entrepreneurs on Fire, The Jenny McCarthy Show, Woman's Day, Los Angeles Business Journal, Entrepreneur, Thrive Global, Selling Power and The Huffington Post.

NoahStJohn.com

Omar Sayed – CEO of Sperse

Omar is the founder of Sperse, a software platform for business management, designed to connect, streamline, and automate critical business functions. Omar's entrepreneurial career in software and marketing has spanned over two decades. His previous company built SiteBuilder.com, a website creation software that powered hundreds of thousands of online stores. As a thought leader in software technologies, Omar helps companies and founders through his advisory roles, partnerships and business acquisitions.

Sperse.com

Pamela Stambaugh – Leadership Expert

Pamela Stambaugh, President and Founder of Accountability Pays Inc., has practiced as a behavioral change master for over 30 years. Today she focuses her attention on emerging leaders with her "Emerging Leader Accelerator" and she supports growing organizations with "CEO Tools by Aprio," the proven step-by-step business system that drives consistent results. CEO stands for Communicate, Execute, Optimize, and over 10,000 managers and CEOs have used CEO Tools to drive profitable growth.

AccountabilityPays.com

Preston Weekes– Chief Strategy Officer of Operations X & Co-Founder of Formula EQ Academy

After starting an auto sales business as a teenager with just one $1,600 car, Preston Weekes built a mega successful car dealership with 15 locations grossing $50 Million in annual sales. Since that early success, he has served as an organizational sales trainer and built training programs including,"Formula X", "Wishes to Riches", "Master Askers", and "You Have A Book In You", and is the co-author of, " How to be up in Down Times." Preston's mission in life is to make the world work for 100% of Humanity and he has served on the boards of several companies including a humanitarian water company. Through his company Operations X, he helps entrepreneurs optimize their operations, minimize expenses, and outsource key functions to low-cost offshore virtual assistants.

OperationsX.com
FormulaEQ.com

Renée Piane – Dating & Relationship Expert

Renée Piane is known around the world as, "The Love Designer". As the pioneer of the first Rapid Dating company in America, Renée has been on a mission teaching, inspiring, and connecting people for over 29 years. Renée is a widely acclaimed inspirational speaker, TV celebrity, radio host, and author of two books, "Get Real about LOVE ~ The Secrets to Opening your Heart & Finding True Love, and Love Mechanics," and "The Power Tools to Build Successful Relationships with Women." She's a role model that mentors people who are looking for love, healing a broken heart, or wanting to reignite the passion in their existing relationships. Her work has been featured on over 75 TV shows and publications including CNN, NBC, ABC, The Today Show, The Wall Street Journal, The Los Angeles Times & The New

York Times. She was voted as the TOP International Dating Coach and was honored to receive the Women's Empowerment Recognition Award.

ReneePiane.com

Robert W. Jones – CEO of iNETrepreneur Network

Robert Jones is the founder of the award-winning INetrepreneur Network, an omni-channel entrepreneurial development organization. Robert's company publishes various collaborative bestselling books and the world class iNETrepreneur Magazine along with the iNETrepreneur Radio Show. His network offers over 1,000 meetings and events per year and is host to the signature event, the Art of Connection Global Summit.

iNETrepreneurNetwork.com

Robin S. Reed – Co-Founder & Partner of EmFluent

Robin is a co-founder and partner at EmFluent, an executive coaching & corporate consulting company that focuses on strategy execution and talent optimization. In addition, Robin serves as the President and CEO of the Black Chamber of Arizona. Robin has been called a "pragmatic visionary" and as entrepreneur at heart, he has demonstrated over his 40-year career where he has started, acquired, operated, and sold several companies.

EmFluent.com

Shea Vaughn – Television Syndication Expert

Shea Vaughn is the founder and CEO of the Worldwide TV Network, an OTT broadcast platform where aspiring hosts can become influential experts, grow their network, and build their brand and credibility from access to over 50 million viewers on leading OTT TV networks, Roku, AppleTV, Chromecast, Google-Plan, Amazon Fire and more. Shea believes in giving people a mix of tools and opportunities, that together with their own faith, it gives them everything need to be successful.

WorldwideTV.tv
WWTVN.com
SheaVaughn.com

Steve Farber – Founder & CEO The Extreme Leadership Institute

Steve is a bestselling author and a seasoned leadership consultant who worked with public and private organizations in virtually every arena. As the former Vice President of legendary management guru Tom Peters' company, Steve is devoted to helping clients develop award-winning cultures and achieve radical results. With over 25 client companies having been ranked on the Best Places to Work list, he's doing things right. His book, "The Radical Leap: A Personal Lesson in Extreme Leadership," was named one of the 100 Best Business Books of All Time. His follow-up books, "The Radical Edge", "Greater Than Yourself", and "Love Is Just Damn Good Business", are highly acclaimed bestsellers featured by the Wall Street Journal, USA Today, Wharton radio and The World Economic Forum. Steve is a member of the Transformational Leadership Council and serves on the board of the Community Alliance for Youth Success, a non-profit organization co-founded by Bobbi DePorter and Stedman Graham.

SteveFarber.com

Steve Rodgers – Spiritual Business Activist

As the former CEO of Real Living Lifestyles and Prudential California Realty, a division of Warren Buffett's Berkshire Hathaway, Steve has lifelong experience in leading businesses and individuals to their highest potential. Steve knows first-hand what it takes to lead and organization of over 4,600 employees, generation $25 billion in annual sales doing nearly 40,000 transactions. One of Steve's career highlights was meeting and working for Warren Buffett for many years. After his wife faced a life-threatening health crisis, Steve shifted his focus to giving back and helping others achieve their dreams. His Amazon best-selling book, "Lead to Gold", shows how to achieve radical personal transformation and break through fear and other challenges. His most recent book, "The IGI Principles", shares seven foundational keystones for Inviting God and Goodness In" to your life and business.

SteveRodgers.net

Stuart Gethner – CEO of Gethner Education Coaching & Consulting

If you are looking for a seasoned real estate investor to help you win, Stuart Gethner is the man you are looking to meet. He has personally invested in over 50 million dollars of income producing real estate and now dedicates his time to helping people build recurring cash flow and financial freedom. Stuart has personally coached hundreds of students on how to successfully invest using seller financing, lease options, whole-saling and fix-&-flips, but his favorite strategy by far is to simply buy and hold to create real wealth.

StuartGethner.com

Thomas Evans – President of HOA.com

Thomas Evans is the co-founder and President of HOA.com the #1 referral network for professionals who serve homeowners. From Realtors to roofers, Thomas is constantly connecting and assisting business owners and professionals with proven strategies to build referral partnerships and attract raving referrals. His passion is helping companies partner and cross-promote each other to expand their mutual revenue and reach. As a U.S. Army combat veteran who served multiple tours in the Middle East, Thomas is passionate about helping veteran-owned businesses grow their businesses and achieve financial freedom.

HOA.com

Tisha Pelletier – Personal Branding Specialist

If you are a solopreneur who is tired of blending into the crowd and looking for a way to stand out and attract new opportunities, then you need to establish your personal brand. As an entrepreneur, Tisha Marie Pelletier knows firsthand how vital building a personal brand is in business. She helps solopreneurs build a strong, standout personal brand within 90 days that's 100% authentic to them, boosts their confidence, and provides the deliverables they need to put their presence out there. Connect with Tisha to book a personal brand strategy session and get access to her Personal Brand Toolkit.

TishaMarie.com

Todd Bookspan - Creator of Win By Noon

Todd is the founder of Win By Noon, a productivity platform and community used by thousands of loan officers and real estate agents to increase their sales. Todd's mission is to teach others how to be mindful and disciplined in their daily activities in order to consistently accomplish their most important priorities and reach their goals. He is also the co-founder of the Modern Mortgage Summit and Modern Real Estate Summit, as well the co-host of the weekly Mortgage Coach Productivity Mastermind and Facebook group.

WinByNoon.com

Tom Crawford – Virtual Healthcare Pioneer

As co-founder of Telehealth Partners and Call A Doctor Plus, Tom Crawford has been at the forefront of virtual healthcare for years. His comprehensive Telehealth platforms help people connect with doctors and medical experts from the comfort of their homes at a fraction of the cost of traditional doctor visits. Tom was the former board chair of Medical Teams International, a non-profit disaster relief organization that uses technology along with "hands on" resources to assist people and provide free healthcare to people in crisis around the world. Tom's vision is to provide free virtual healthcare to everyone on the planet.

TelehealthPartners.com

Tom Gay – CEO of TribeUp.com

Tom Gay is the founder and CEO of TribeUp.com. TribeUp helps business professionals attract, invite, engage, manage and monetize their relationships and networks. Over his storied career, Tom has trained many thousands of professionals on growing their success through a systematic way to gain referrals. Working side by side with clients for many years, Tom is passionate about helping people bring relationships and collaboration back into their lives and business. He does this through a new, "by invitation only," globally growing SaaS platform to help people get out of digital/ social media noise and back to building their trusted "tribes."

WhyTribeUp.com

Dr. Tony Alessandra – Founder of Assessments 24x7

Dr. Tony Alessandra realized success as a graduate professor of marketing, internet entrepreneur, business author, and keynote speaker. He is the founder of Assessments 24x7 LLC, a company that offers a variety of online assessments, including the widely used DISC profile and HireSense assessment. As the author of over 30 books, Dr. Alessandra was inducted into the National Speakers Association "Speakers Hall of Fame" in 1985 and the Legends of the Speaking Profession in 2009.

Alessandra.com
Assessments24x7.com
DrTonyVirtualTraining.com

National Networking Organizations & Resources

Alignable

Alignable is a free online business network for small business owners across North America. Members use Alignable to connect within their local business community or in other markets across the country. Members can access industry insights and share updates about their business. While this is a great platform to connect with people online, you will need to take your conversations into the real world if you hope to build solid referral partnerships through this platform.

Alignable.com

Biz To Biz Global Networking

Biz to Biz was founded in 2006 by Tracy Kienitz whose goal is to empower small businesses to thrive against the high odds of failure. They operate networking groups in Montana, Washington, Minnesota, Utah, and Colorado providing business mentorship in a positive community environment. Their groups are known for quality connections of people committed to helping small business owners and professionals gain more referrals and grow their business. If you are looking for access to a community of people who are in it to win it, check out Biz to Biz Global Networking.

Biztobiznow.com

BNI Business Networking International

BNI is the world's leading business referral organization with over 280,000 Members in over 10,000 BNI Chapters worldwide. In 2020 alone, BNI Members shared over 11.5 million valuable new client referrals and generated over $16.2B (USD) in revenue. Many BNI Chapters are currently meeting using BNI Online™, a powerful and convenient platform that enables Members to continue sharing new client referrals. BNI Members are actively supported by regional, national, and global BNI staff that provide the training, structure, and the technology needed for the continued success of BNI Members. Each chapter allows just one person to represent each professional category. This gives participants exclusivity in their area of service helping them connect and collaborate with complementary business owners and professionals.

BNI.com

C-Suite Network

C-Suite Network™ prides itself as the world's most trusted network of C-Suite Leaders, with a focus on providing growth, development, and networking opportunities for business executives with titles of Vice President and above with annual revenues of $5 million or greater. The C-Suite Network helps create lasting business relationships, connections, and insights among senior leaders. Their focus is to serve executives who want to come into a trusted community and use content to grow their business, influence, and reach.

C-SuiteNetwork.com

Eventbrite

Although not a networking organization, Eventbrite is an online platform listing live events and experiences in your local market. Their mission is to bring the world together through live experiences. Here you can search for and find local business and networking opportunities led by local chambers of entrepreneurs.

Eventbrite.com

eWomen Network

For women looking to connect with other entrepreneurial women, check out the eWomenNetwork. If you're looking to launch, grow and scale your business, they offer Accelerated Networking™ at over 2,000 online and in-person events each year. You'll find customers, innovative ideas, and breakthrough resources to help you succeed. The eWomen Network's mission is to help one million women entrepreneurs each achieve one million dollars in annual revenue They connect more than 500,000 women entrepreneurs through 118 local chapters across North America

providing members with resources, networking, marketing, promotion, coaching, events, podcasts, speaking, scholarships, grants, video production, and more to help grow their businesses.
eWomenNetwork.com

Happy Networking Project

The Happy Networking Project is a newer organization formed to facilitate virtual online networking events. Their mission is to make Happy Neighborhood Project the happiest place in the world for business just like Disney is the happiest place for children. They give people opportunities to be local leaders facilitating online groups to help you find resources and connections to move your business forward.

HappyNeighborhoodProject.com

HOA.com

HOA.com is the #1 referral network for professionals who serve homeowners. The vision that began as "The Home Owner Alliance" quickly expanded once the domain HOA.com was secured in 2020. Now this national network unites tens of thousands of top trusted contractors, Realtors, and other home services businesses and professionals who provide services specific to homeowners. The company has high service standards professionals must meet in order to qualify as Certified Pros and Premier Pros. They also offer a Preferred Partner program for larger companies that have the capacity to serve a larger service area. A unique feature of this network is that they have Referral Partner Managers who actively assist their Certified Pros and

Premier Pros in creating strong referral partnerships to generate referrals for years to come. If you or your business serves homeowners, has been in business at least five years with a majority of 5-star reviews, visit HOA.com/premier to apply for their powerful and profitable partner program.

HOA.com

iNETrepreneur Network

The iNETrepreneur Network offers an omni-channel ecosystem solution for entrepreneurs, business owners, and influencers, who look to leverage traditional, personal, and digital marketing through business networking, public speaking, and education globally. Based in Phoenix, AZ, their community of entrepreneurs place value on relationships with community members gaining access to more than 1,200 meetings, events, and academy classes throughout the year. What's different about this networking group is that you can contribute articles and advertise in their iNETrepreneur Magazine, attend and learn from their iNETrepreneur Academy, speak from the stage at in-person or virtual events, or be interviewed on the iNETrepreneur Radio Show. Truly an integrative approach to connecting and business networking.

iNETrepreneurNetwork.com

LeTip

LeTip International is the oldest and one of the most trusted business networking groups in the country. They truly are the business referral network that started it all. LeTip prides itself on building more than just strong business relationships. Their business networking group cultivates a lifetime business networking group model based on building, sustaining, and supporting strong relationships between businesspeople. LeTip members form a close-knit family of non-competing businesses. LeTip Business Networking Group Chapter members spend time learning about each other's business, powering their ability to make better referrals. By becoming well-versed in each other's industries, they can make higher-quality referrals. These high level tips turn their local business referral network chapters into powerful and result driven sales forces.

LeTip.com

MeetUp

Meetup is a platform for finding and building local events and communities. People use Meetup to meet new people, learn new things, find support, get out of their comfort zones, and pursue their passions together. Check out local events, join a group to meet people, make friends, find support, grow a business, and explore your interests. Thousands of events are happening every day , both online and in person so it's a great place to get connected in your local community.

MeetUp.com

Network After Work

Network After Work is America's premier face-to-face business networking company with monthly mixer events in over 85+ cities catering to 6 million members. Attendees make valuable connections with other members of their business community while enjoying different exciting venues including clubs, restaurants, hotels, and special event locations. Network After Work launched in 2009 and has become the largest and fastest growing organization of its kind. Each event attracts a diverse mix of up to several hundred professionals from all industries and career levels. It all takes place on a week day right after work in a fun and relaxed atmosphere conducive to making connections.

NetworkAfterWork.com

Network In Action

Network In Action International believes that the perfect mix of technology and face to face networking will help your business grow. All Network In Action groups have only one mandatory monthly meeting as opposed to a weekly obligation. Their mobile app helps keep you connected throughout the month, potentially freeing up over 80 hours a year so that you can focus on what's important: Growing your business. Check their website to explore their various chapters across the United States.

NetworkInAction.com

One Business Connection

Since 1997, One Business Connection (1BC) has been connecting and empowering business owners and professionals. From their headquarters in Denver, CO, 1BC prides itself on being a success organization that puts you in contact with the connections, the ideas, and the people you need to grow your business. 1BC is committed to helping their members grow both personally and professionally providing its own success library on success, motivation, and inspiration.

OneBusiness.com

Pod.io

Pod.io is a mobile app with an interactive map featuring their 5 million members. Create your free profile and connect with other business owners and professionals in your local market. Search by profession and see people in your own community who could be strong referral partners for your business. With over 250,000 real estate professionals in the network, there are extensive opportunities to grow your business by connecting with quality people.

Pod.io

TEAM Referral Network

TEAM Referral Network was created in 2002 out of La Verne, California. The organization has since grown to over 100 chapters across California, Washington, Colorado, and Missouri. TEAM Referral Network includes weekly meetings with your chapter, training programs, business development, and most importantly, quality business relationships. Members are encouraged to meet one-on-one with other members to get to know each other on a deeper level. The entire TEAM Referral Network has access to all members with the exclusive TEAM sponsored member's website. These "mini" websites give added value to your brand's online presence and search engine rankings (SEO), as well as make it even easier for prospects to find your company online. TEAM Referral Network also provides regular business development trainings, as well as their annual "Big Event", where keynote speakers and coaches challenge you to go to the next level with your business.

TeamReferralNetwork.com

TribeUp

This platform provides a proven process to build your tribe, grow your influence, and create win-win-win outcomes. Their technology and tools help you attract and invite all your contacts into your personal tribe where you can engage with them in a collaborative, conscious and responsible way. You can get started as a free "Tribe Guest" then once you complete the orientation training you can get verified and approved to become a "Tribe Member". Once you are an approved Tribe Member you gain access to prebuilt resources to attract and expand your tribe including a unique personal invite link that allows you to invite contacts directly into your tribe and places them in the powerful Tribe Relationship Manager (TRM) tool.

"Tribe Builders" have access to powerful publishing tools to post their offers, content, and events that can be found by other "Tribe Guests" and above. They can also be converted into tribe building invite links to grow your tribe.

TribeUp.com

Vistage

While not a traditional networking organization, Vistage is the world's largest executive coaching organization for small and mid-size businesses. For more than 60 years they've been helping CEOs, business owners and key executives solve their toughest challenges through a comprehensive approach to success. At the heart of their formula is confidential peer advisory groups and executive coaching sessions.

If you are looking to connect with successful business leaders, Vistage is a great organization to participate in.

Vistage.com

Women Speakers Association

The Women Speakers Association (WSA) is the first ever global gathering place for women speakers, authors, and experts to support, mastermind and mentor one another to take a collective and powerful stance in ushering in the voice of the 21st Century Woman. Since 2011, WSA has been THE go to place for innovative leaders, change agents, and women with a message to connect, collaborate, and grow their visibility worldwide. WSA features members in 120 countries with an online presence that reaches millions. Whatever your "stage" is, be it a virtual classroom, a boardroom, the floor of the U.N., an internet radio show, physical stage, or any other platform, WSA is dedicated to empowering you to authentically express yourself, build a thriving, prosperous business, and cause serious transformation in the lives of your clients, companies, communities, and the world. Their vision is of a world in which women are empowered to authentically express themselves; to build a thriving, prosperous business; and feel a part of something greater. If you are a woman looking to share your message with the world, there's no better place I know to help you connect, collaborate, and empower others together.

WomenSpeakersAssociation.com

Become A Raving Referrals Co-Author

If you love what you've read and are interested in elevating your credibility and visibility by being a featured co-author in one of our upcoming industry related *Raving Referrals* books, we want to hear from you. We're looking for quality experts and influencers with subject matter expertise in the following areas:

- Raving Referrals for Accountants
- Raving Referrals for Attorneys
- Raving Referrals for B2B Sales
- Raving Referrals for Business Coaches
- Raving Referrals for Car Sales People
- Raving Referrals for Charities
- Raving Referrals for Chiropractors
- Raving Referrals for Dentists
- Raving Referrals for Doctors
- Raving Referrals for Electricians
- Raving Referrals for Financial Advisors
- Raving Referrals for General Contrators
- Raving Referrals for Home Service Pros
- Raving Referrals for Insurance Agents
- Raving Referrals for Life Coaches

- Raving Referrals for Marketing Consultants
- Raving Referrals for Mortgage Pros
- Raving Referrals for Network Marketers
- Raving Referrals for Orthodontists
- Raving Referrals for Painters
- Raving Referrals for Personal Trainers
- Raving Referrals for Plumbers
- Raving Referrals for Realtors
- Raving Referrals for Veterinarians

To begin a conversation and explore the possibilities of partnership on an upcoming *Raving Referrals* book, call (602) 693-1763 or go to RavingReferrals.com/coauthor.

Become A Raving Referrals Certified Trainer

Are you ready to take the stage and empower people to have more income, more influence, and more impact?

Then consider getting trained and approved as a *Raving Referrals Certified Trainer*. This program helps solidify your knowledge and mastery of attracting *Raving Referrals*. It also propels your credibility and visibility and opens new income streams to unlock the financial freedom you desire and deserve.

As a *Raving Referrals Certified Trainer*, you have the opportunity to:

- Create powerful and profitable referral partnerships
- Win more clients as a trusted expert in your local market
- Be an influential local leader in the world's fastest growing referral network
- Earn lucrative recurring commissions for years to come

Sharing our program with local professionals and businesses can help you attract more clients for your business, while adding a lucrative long-term income stream.

Ideal candidates exude the following qualities:

- Charismatic
- Inspiring Leader
- Passionate Promoter
- Natural Networker
- Well Connected
- Highly Respected
- Deeply Involved in Your Community
- Actively Serves in Your Charity or Church
- Master of Consultative Sales
- Confident Public Speaker/Trainer
- Active User of Social Media
- Has Existing Fans & Followers
- Participates in a Networking Group

Experience in these professions preferred:

- Business Coaches & Consultants
- Business Focused Service Providers
- Corporate Speakers & Trainers
- Home Service Professionals
- Marketing Consultants
- Mortgage Pros
- Real Estate Salespeople

To learn more about this powerful program, call (602) 693-1763 or go to RavingReferrals.com/certification.

About The Author

Brandon Barnum, often referred to as the "King of Referrals," is an award-winning serial entrepreneur, coach, consultant, speaker, trainer, and workshop leader. He serves as CEO of HOA.com – the #1 Referral Network for Home Service Professionals, and as the Chairman of the Board for The Champions Institute.

He is a highly sought-after expert in referrals, marketing, sales, joint ventures, business development, and business growth strategies.

While a single Dad, in 1997, Brandon was an early technology innovator featuring real estate property listings from Realtors that he partnered with and promoted.

After learning the art and science of referrals, he increased his annual income 10X from 20K to $200K in just 18 months. Brandon has since closed over $500 million in transactions by referrals and has founded multiple local and online referral platforms and networks connecting 5 million members in 195 countries.

Upon learning the B.A.N.K. sales methodology, Brandon helped launch and served as CEO of Codebreaker Technologies, building *Codebreaker AI* for sales. He now helps businesses close more sales in less time, training the B.A.N.K. sales methodology through his training and coaching company, The Champions Institute.

Brandon has been featured internationally on TV, radio, and several books, including *Cracking the Millionaire Code* and *Zero to Hero*, and in magazines including The *Wall Street Journal, Business Journal*, and *Newsweek*, to name a few.

Brandon is passionate about empowering business owners and professionals with a step-by-step system for attracting profitable prospects and expanding their income, influence, and impact.

To contact Brandon for executive coaching, workshops or keynote speaking:

Phone: **602-693-1763**
Email: brandon@RavingReferrals.com
Web: www.RavingReferrals.com
LinkedIn: www.linkedin.com/in/brandonbarnum/

We invite you to leave a review of this book on Amazon and Goodreads

Made in the USA
Las Vegas, NV
27 June 2022